WINNING RESEARCH FUNDING

This book is dedicated to my colleagues in a vibrant and vital academic community, to those who fund our research and to all who are affected by the outcomes.

WINNING RESEARCH FUNDING

Abby Day Peters

GOWER

Published by
Gower Publishing Limited
Gower House
Croft Road
Aldershot
Hampshire GU11 3HR
England

Gower Publishing Company
Suite 420
101 Cherry Street
Burlington VT 05401–4405
USA

Abby Day Peters has asserted her right under the Copyright, Designs and Patents Act 1988 to be identified as the author of this work.

British Library Cataloguing in Publication Data
Peters, Abby Day, 1956–
   Winning research funding
   1. Research – Finance
   I. Title
   001.4'4

ISBN 0-566-08459-7

Library of Congress Cataloging-in-Publication Data
Peters, Abby Day, 1956–
   Winning research funding / Abby Day Peters.
      p. cm.
   ISBN 0-566-08459-7 (pbk.: alk. paper)
      1. Research grants. 2. Proposal writing for grants. I. Title.

HG177.P474 2003
001.4'4–dc21   2002032666

Typeset in 10pt Plantin Light by IML Typographers, Birkenhead and printed in Great Britain by MPG Books Ltd., Bodmin, Cornwall.

CONTENTS

LIST OF TABLES

PREFACE

The most influential people in the world base their decisions on research findings. Education ministers, vice chancellors, world leaders, chief executives, professors, charity trustees, clergymen, scientists, journalists – anyone in a position of institutional, structural power will make important decisions by first asking: what do we know about this? For a government minister, it means obtaining evidence and argument to guide a policy decision; for a chief executive, it is understanding the background and consequences of an investment; for a professor, it is a matter of remaining current with the body of knowledge; for a director of a charitable trust, it means honouring the benefactor's request to help humanity.

The people who struggle with questions and issues, who try to develop an understanding of and answers to important questions, who inform and guide decisions which affect everyone's future are some of the most important people in the world. These people are 'researchers'. Researchers access, develop, create and eventually embody the knowledge so desperately needed by those who take and shape decisions.

But this kind of research doesn't just happen. Some people are prepared to pay for knowledge to be created. We'll call them 'funders'. These 'funders' are not hobbyists with nothing better to do than indulge their whims: they are committed to the principles they want to fund. We will discuss these funding bodies in detail in this book. Some are government or education department agencies; some charitable trusts, dedicated to using vast legacies left, often many years ago, to further knowledge for the public good. Some are for-profit corporations, who see scholarly research as an important, if indirect way, to benefit long-term shareholder value.

Funders need researchers as much as researchers need them. What, for example, would happen to a funding council which consistently failed to attract high quality researchers? How would a charity explain to its trustees that its enormous pile of money is gathering dust and interest because they cannot distribute it to worthy researchers? How would directors of research or corporate affairs explain to colleagues and shareholders that they have failed to find people to help develop cutting-edge theory or counter-intuitive conceptual thinking? Funders are not doing researchers a favour. They are deeply indebted to and dependent upon the researchers they support.

Yet, of all the thousands of applications and proposals researchers send to funders each year, most are rejected. This represents a gross waste of time and money on everyone's part. The researcher – usually an underpaid, over-worked academic – has wasted weeks and months preparing an unsuccessful proposal. For a contract researcher, time spent composing rejected proposals is an unpaid effort. The people assessing the proposal – usually underpaid, over-worked academics themselves – have spent months and sometimes years trying to find the right researchers. Most of those who sit on advisory councils and research panels, for example, are not paid at all. They are from academe, government, and the private sector and are acting out of commitment and interest. They, like the researchers who apply, believe passionately in the field they represent. How can so many like-minded people fail to forge mutually beneficial relationships?

This book addresses and, I hope, resolves that problem.

Research Method

The suggestions and stories here were gleaned from in-depth interviews and literature searches over a ten-month period. My objective was to tease out people's experiences and judgements about research funding, to try to go beyond the usual pro-forma approach and discover the informal structures and, most importantly, the tacit rules of the game.

As one academic researcher put it:

> I think the real thing is knowing how the rules
> really work, rather than the sort of open rules.
> And I think that only comes from experience
> and I think that's why a lot of people say – if
> you've been successful in the past, you're
> more likely to be successful in the future. The
> sponsoring body deny that, but I think that is
> inevitable because if you've been successful in
> the past, you know how things work, so you're
> more likely to be successful in the future.

And so I talked with people who are successful in obtaining research funding, as well as those who fund them: people from research councils, government, university departments, the private sector, contract researchers, charitable foundations and trusts.

My methods included:

- taped, semi-structured face-to-face interviews
- untaped, semi-structured face-to-face interviews
- semi-structured telephone interviews
- informal, unstructured conversations over lunch/coffee/drinks
- e-mail conversations derived from web research
- literature searches
- informal conversations at conferences

In most cases the clarity and illuminating quality of the words used by my interviewees enabled me to use their words intact to illustrate good practice in winning research funding.

ADP

ACKNOWLEDGEMENTS

Like any piece of research, this book is a product of collaboration. Without so many people's time, interest and willingness to share it would have remained simply an idea.

But a brilliant idea at that. I would like to say I had thought of it myself but, truthfully, full credit goes entirely to the publisher and particularly to Jo Burges at Gower. Being a published author with Gower, I already knew Jo and respected her eye and judgement, but I was nevertheless initially taken aback by the audacity of her suggestion. Was there really a secret to being funded, and particularly one that wouldn't compromise academic ideals and integrity?

This book is the result of that idea and Jo's persistence in following the story. I am grateful for her support, professionalism and enthusiasm which sustained the project from its conception to completion. On the topic of conception, I am also grateful to Guy Loft at Gower who took over from Jo when she embarked on maternity leave. The book was nearly complete by then but it was his onerous responsibility to act as midwife during some occasionally protracted final stages.

This work has been informed, not primarily by desk research and web crawls, but by the people whose livelihoods depend on research funding. That includes people who want funding and people whose job it is to generate and distribute it.

I decided to start my research on the topic by talking with people who had won research funding and who would be willing to share their stories. From there, I moved into the realm of the funders themselves and talked to people with years of experience vetting and managing researchers. I was quickly gratified that they all seemed to tell the same story: winning research funding is a matter of the attitude one brings to the task. Beyond the 'top tips', which of course I included here, there was something else, something about working with people and forming relationships. This seemed to apply equally to a single researcher wanting money for a small project to a large, international research team.

For their insights and enthusiasm I gained in interviews, meetings, correspondence and presentations I am particularly indebted to: Elizabeth Atherton, Peter Brown, Chris Caswill, David Crowther, Rosalind Edwards, Ken Emond, Jacqui Forsyth, Yvonne Fox, Howard Green, Bob Gomersall, Mathew Guest, Yvonne Hawkins, Clarissa Hughes, Cathy Hick, Jane Hunt, Zahir Irani, Janet Lewis, Peter Nolan, Simon Kerridge, Phil Macnaghten, Steve Morgan, Martin Penny, Alan Prout, Rod Rhodes, Sharon Witherspoon, Bronislaw Szerszynski, Peter Townsend, Karin Tusting, Jeffrey Williams, Catrin Wood, Linda Woodhead, and Mohamed Zairi.

To the British Academy, and in particular Jonathan Breckon and Carol Marsh, many thanks indeed for organising with RAGnet a most productive workshop on research funding in April 2002. It provided many people with a unique opportunity to speak directly to representatives from major funding organisations and allowed me to present the findings from my book and gain feedback.

Angela Clow and her colleagues from the Department of Psychology at the University of Westminster gave me my first opportunity to lead a workshop on winning research funding in June 2002. It was kind and brave of them to act as 'guinea pigs', testing out the concepts and practicalities that run through this book. I am grateful for their contributions and warm response.

My most heartfelt thanks to my children, Alexandra and Jake, who are ever-patient with a mother who is sometimes too long at the computer, and to John Peters. Besides being the best editor I've ever worked with, his support and constructive evaluation made all the difference between a job and a joy.

ADP

PART *I*

YOUR RESEARCH FOCUS

1 WHY DO WE NEED FUNDED RESEARCH?

Top Tips

When I asked people how research funding is won, I received generally two types of responses. The first is what I would call the 'top tip' list.

I asked everyone I interviewed to name, in brief, a few important factors: those which really make the difference between a winning proposal and a lower-quality one. They clustered, conveniently, under ten broad headings (see Table 1.1 below). These 'ten top tips' will be explored through the book.

Table 1.1   Ten Top Tips for winning research funding

```
 1. Articulates problem accurately
 2. Provides appropriate background
 3. Manageable within the time
 4. Cost-effective
 5. Linked to defined outcomes
 6. Seen to make a contribution to the field
 7. Clear methodology
 8. Concise writing
 9. Demonstrates right team approach
10. Has credible academic supervision
```

While the list in Table 1.1 may seem obvious good practice, these success factors are often ignored by people who fail to win funding. This may reflect their inexperience or time pressures. We will be discussing these factors in detail, and offering the benefit of many people's experiences.

Yet beyond those process-related issues is another question: why, all other things being equal, are some researchers more successful than others? It does not seem enough to simply do well; it is necessary to do better than that. What is the meaning of that 'better'? In other words, what, in research, is best practice?

Research Best Practice

Some people say it is factors outside the applicant's control that makes the difference. Examples of such comments are:

● Themes are designated each year by research councils – how can you know in advance what they will be?
● A proposal just may not have the right 'fit' with the funder.
● Referees may not like you! You may have offended them previously. It's a small world and even so-called blind refereeing processes may be transparent. As one referee remarked: 'It's easy to tell who the authors are – they're the ones most frequently referenced.'

Several people told me that it is a matter of luck. But what is luck? Should we abandon the quest for best practice in favour of astrology? The following is a typical response to my question 'but what is luck?'

> Well, I mean, there's always a bit of luck. You haven't got a sort of magic ball to see in the future. You can actually anticipate that this has got the conditions likely to lead to controversy, but it doesn't mean that controversy is likely to occur. I mean, of course you can't, but you can have good hunches and our hunches in fact were correct at the time.

We will be illustrating how successful applicants for research funding convert those 'hunches' into what they really are: reasonable judgements built up over time in a field of expertise. We look at how to develop those 'hunches' into winning research relationships.

Of course, there is always a measure of good fortune in any endeavour. Sometimes it is a matter of being in the right place at the right time or hitting the right tone with the right person on the right day. But most of the time it is more than luck.

People who win research funding and the people who write the cheques agree that for most applicants most of the time luck is not the most important factor: *people who win research funding consistently take a different and measurably better approach than those who do not.* That 'approach' is something more complex than simply filling out an application form properly, wearing decent clothes for an interview, carefully reading a call for tender, designing a research approach or writing clearly. Clearly, the Top Ten Tips are necessary, but often insufficient, conditions of success.

That leads me to the second sort of response I received. Most successful researchers talk more about relationships, proactivity and partnerships than they do about applications and proposals. This means that researchers need to choose a prospective funder who matches their needs and interests. To work effectively, the relationship needs to be symmetrical and symbiotic.

Unbalanced relationships are flawed from the outset. Recognising this, many funders choose not to work with researchers whose focus and approach are not compatible with theirs. That is a reasonable and fair decision. Researchers who seek funding from such inappropriate organisations are likely to be disappointed, even if they receive the money they were looking for. Janet Lewis, recently retired Research Director of the Joseph Rowntree Foundation, summarised this approach as collaboration:

> The message I give when I go round and talk
> to people about putting in proposals is that
> you need to think really hard about what
> you're doing. If someone works at putting in a
> good proposal, and it is funded, we will want
> to work in a collaborative way with them, but
> not all of them want that. Some people hate
> the idea of having an advisory group. They
> think – how dare anybody try to tell me how
> to do my work? Advisory groups for those
> projects never work. The only way they can
> work, and it's absolutely wonderful when they
> do, is if people are willing to work in that
> collaborative kind of way.

Based on the assumption that research funding can represent mutual long-term benefit to both partners, this book takes a strategic approach. Whether your desired funding is for a small grant or a five-year programme, it is likely you will be spending a significant amount of time on your research and, consequently, on obtaining the funding. In many cases, you will also be involved with your funder during the research and following. This book aims to help you create a context, a process and an approach which will make those partnerships worthwhile and enjoyable.

Book Structure

The book is structured in four main parts, each reflecting an important part of the process and partnership. The first part acts as a review of what you are doing and why, to help you focus on what will be the most important aspects of your work to you and to your potential funder.

One of the strongest temptations challenging those who want funding is to jump into the application stage without thinking through what they are doing and why. We will examine in more detail the question about why research funding is important. Not everyone needs it and not everyone wants it. We look at research issues, not only from your perspective but also from that of the funders and other stakeholders.

Identifying the issues is an important step, but many researchers resist articulating precisely why the issue is important and to whom. This is the great 'so what?' question that needs to be answered in simple, clear terms. That is why we look at implications and outcomes. Why is the research important, and to whom? There are a number of potential answers.

The research may, for example:

- add conceptually to the current body of knowledge through new thinking
- add empirically to the current body of knowledge through new evidence
- expose and correct an error which has been compounded over the years by researchers who failed to see it
- demonstrate a new way of applying the body of knowledge
- help an organisation work differently and better.

Even when the themes and priorities have been articulated by the funding body, it is the researcher's task to identify the implications and the result. If it will add conceptually to the body of knowledge, how will that knowledge be different from what exists already and why is it important? How will it be disseminated? If the implication is that an organisation's current working practices should change, how will that new thinking be accessed by the organisation? Will there be books? Papers? Seminars? When? How many?

Funding bodies, public or private, want to see value for money. The researcher who receives funding needs to demonstrate that it will be used appropriately and that the investment will be worthwhile.

Many proposals do successfully address the issues and their implications but still fail. This is usually because the researcher has not explained fully how the research will be carried out – a common reason for rejection. Some proposals do not detail a research method at all, or provide only the barest description. This leaves the potential funder with two concerns:

- An inappropriate method that does not address the research issue may mean the applicant does not understand the research issue.
- A sparse description of method means the applicant has not thought about how to conduct the research and is therefore either incapable or uninterested.

Sometimes, funders may specify a method or underlying assumptions with which the researcher disagrees. Researchers often feel they need to challenge what is being proposed. How best to respond to that – without alienating the potential funder – is discussed in detail. Potential funders need to be convinced that the researcher will carry out the research professionally and ethically. They also understand that, in practice, some elements of research design will change as the research unfolds. Researchers need to specify the method in some detail, including the areas which may change with circumstances or findings.

And how will you know if it's any good? Good research is a matter of perspective, with different people having different definitions based on their background and their needs. Researchers can benefit from addressing the wider range of qualitative judgements about what constitutes 'good research'.

The final chapter of Part I examines the mechanics of the research. Who will conduct the research? How much will it cost? The funder is looking here not for convenience or economy, but – once again – for value. Is the research team sufficiently capable to finish the project according to specification? Is the costing realistic? Sometimes, applications fail because the budget is beyond anything the funder can meet, but they also fail because the cost estimates are unrealistically low. Those who fund research do not evaluate proposals based on a notion that 'cheapest is best'. They are, by and large, experienced and committed people with good judgement about likely returns on investment, likelihood of successful completion, and the right balance of costs and benefits. Poor budgeting – either too high or too low – may suggest that the applicant has not reviewed the project carefully, or is too inexperienced to complete it successfully.

The second part takes a closer look at how funding bodies work and what motivates them, to help you assess which may be a well-suited partner. Too many researchers rush around looking for a funding partner in a panic-stricken attempt to find money. Many do not find one or, worse (in the long run), find one who is not suitable. What do you really want, and who will want you?

This is the time to think about what you can gain from a research partnership and what you can give. What benefits are you seeking and how will the relationship benefit both you and your potential funder? The most obvious, but least interesting, benefit is money. Most successful researchers are motivated by more than money: cash is just one fuel that keeps the project running.

Funders talk more about 'value' than they do about money. Thinking more qualitatively than quantitatively puts the idea of value in a different perspective. Professor Mohamed Zairi, Director of the European Centre for Total Quality Management at Bradford University, says it is wrapped up in the role of the academic scholar:

> It's not just a question of process, about how to do it, how you go about getting access to companies and putting bids for monies and getting funded posts like a Chair or a lectureship. It's not about process. I think it's about relationships first of all, and in order to make relationships work I think we need to become humble and fundamentally re-examine our role as academics. It's about integrity, pride, partnerships and the principle of value.

The need to deliver value applies to all potential funders, not just the corporate sector. We look in more detail at particular kinds of funders: government, research councils, the European Community, charitable foundations, and professional bodies. Is it possible to have a long-term relationship with what some people perceive as a faceless bureaucracy? By listening to those who claim they do, we can learn that there is no such thing as facelessness – only organisations composed of people, many of them academics, who are as inspired by emerging research questions and complex problems as any researcher. Getting to know these people and how they work is a necessary step in forging long-term relationships.

There is a separate chapter on working with the corporate sector, reflecting an increasing trend for academic researchers to work with private enterprise. Some of the relationships we describe demonstrate unexpected alliances. Why, for example, is a green-oriented environmental researcher involved with one of the world's largest global capitalists? Dr Phil Macnaghten, from the Centre for the Study of Environmental Change at Lancaster University (CSEC), explains:

> The reason we got involved with Unilever
> was a marriage of interests. It was really an
> early attempt to think about wider issues of
> corporate social responsibility.

Some people worry that such relationships sully academic standards and compromise academic integrity. Why should they? All researchers are paid by somebody. We find here that the qualities which the corporate sector value most highly from academics is their integrity, rigour and credibility. Those who deliver those qualities are respected and their work applied to what is often ground-breaking, world-changing activities.

That does not, however, mean it is right for everyone to seek corporate funding. The cultures of academe and the corporate world are very different and, for some, unbridgeable. Differences in time-scales, vocabulary, expectations and presentation are explored here.

The third part talks about building the relationship. How will you know if this is the right partner and you can meet their expectations? Assessing a potential partner's needs does not need to be a difficult task. Unfortunately, it is one most often ignored and said to be the most common cause of application rejection: 'we often wonder if academics can read,' one funder said bluntly.

To put it a little more gently, 'Don't be afraid of presenting your ideas in a way that reflects the interests of the funders as well as your own,' suggests Mathew Guest, a research associate at Durham University who has successfully won research funding in the past. He elaborates:

> Obtaining funding is an exercise in 'selling' a
> project or set of ideas to an audience that has
> a particular set of interests. Within the
> context of such a process, there is an
> inevitable degree of compromise, as projects
> – or at least their initial outline – are adjusted
> in accordance with the stated priorities of
> funding bodies.

Uncovering needs may also be more complex, particularly when working with the corporate sector. This may mean creating opportunities to familiarise yourself with the area, such as reading their journals and attending conferences. It will also mean talking with people, perhaps informally at first, to assess what they really need. Maintaining the position of 'relationship' means this is a valuable, enquiring process. Following through the marriage metaphor, it is a time to get to know each other before taking the relationship to any formal stage.

This continues into how the relationship develops. Sometimes, research partnerships break down because each party has different expectations. This will apply to the process of carrying out the research as well as its outcomes. How do academics respond when the research question in a call for tender is clearly wrong, or the proposed methodology inappropriate? We explore here how to meet the funder's expectations without compromising your own values or preferred approach.

The task of preparing a proposal and, sometimes, making a presentation follows. Writing and presenting a proposal is unlikely to be rewarded if researchers skip the preparation stages described above. The proposal and a presentation is one stage in the process of successfully winning research funding, not the whole of the process. Part III incorporates ideas and advice from successful researchers about how to create the right tone and achieve the final touch of finesse that may make the difference between your submission and a hundred others.

Some processes include a phase of feedback where the funder proposes changes or demands reductions in time and money. Consider this part of the relationship, an iterative process enriched by negotiation and amendment. It is often here that the greatest benefit of an open mind is appreciated. In some cases, responding to a request for a change leads to more money, not less: it is not always bad news. Feedback from a proposal is free, often excellent, advice.

In Part IV, we examine how the relationship and your profile develops through time. Most people who succeed find that the next application is easier and more likely to be approved. Many do not have to search again for research partners because the partners are coming to them. Successful researchers spend less time applying for funding or submitting tenders – they are the ones often consulted by the funding body about how to create the tender. They are often given the first opportunity to consider funding before anyone else. As the relationship develops, both researcher and funder may find opportunities come as easily as picking up the phone. None of this, however, happens by accident. Successful relationships are nurtured. Knowing how to manage the research partnership will often involve new skills and new ways of working.

It is critical to future projects that the current one is successful. Who sets the evaluation criteria and how can you influence it? With research councils, new people are often brought into the project to evaluate its success. How can you continue to exert an influence on the process? In the private sector, using the right language and orientation can make all the difference between what you, and they, see as successful. As one academic put it: 'You need to translate what is academically interesting to what is commercially useful.'

One of the necessary outcomes of most research projects is publication. This is something which the funder may or may not require; some may even prohibit it, others may demand it. How do researchers satisfy the need to publish within this complex context? This becomes increasingly difficult in an environment where contract research is more prevalent. Here, every moment counts, every day is billed. Sadly, few days if any can be billed for publication.

Researchers who successfully manage both research and writing plan for publication from the outset. It is easier to think through prospective publication routes when the research is fresh and thriving than when it is finished and growing stale. Here, we focus on overcoming the most common reason for papers being rejected – poor targeting. Most papers are rejected simply because they are sent to the wrong place. We look at how to choose the right journal and how to widen the dissemination plan to ensure you are being seen in the right places for future funders.

Finally, we'll consider how much time you really need to spend writing a paper. A year? A month? A few days? Writing better and writing faster are key skills for researchers who hope to position themselves for future funding. Some funding bodies search for researchers who will suit their needs. Tracking published papers, they say, is the most common way of finding the right people.

Research and the Researcher

The researcher is one of the most important people in society. Researchers influence decisions and, in so doing, influence lives. As well as providing useful knowledge and informing policy and corporate decisions, they influence how we measure and value the outcomes of research itself.

This book has been written to make their task easier and more fruitful, to understand 'luck' for what it really is – careful positioning and astute judgement. That, more than anything, is what takes the researcher to the right place and the right people at the right time.

The book's central proposition is that there is poor, good and best practice in research funding today. In exploring best practice we need to go further than our Top Ten Tips list in Table 1.1. Those are, indeed, the structural components of research best practice, but not its foundation.

Winning research funding consistently depends on concepts like value and partnership. These concepts turn a one-off experience into a long-term, mutually satisfying relationship where both partners benefit equally. The benefits extend far beyond money to prestige, knowledge and influence.

2 WHY LOOK FOR RESEARCH FUNDING?

What is Research?

Research includes a broad range of activities. As UK institutions depend heavily on the outcome of the Research Assessment Exercise (RAE) for funding, the definition of research it provides is probably most relevant. Their 2001 RAE guidelines defines research as:

> 'Research' for the purpose of the RAE is to be understood as original investigation undertaken in order to gain knowledge and understanding. It includes work of direct relevance to the needs of commerce and industry, as well as to the public and voluntary sectors; scholarship;[1] the invention and generation of ideas, images, performances and artefacts including design, where these lead to new or substantially improved insights; and the use of existing knowledge in experimental development to produce new or substantially improved materials, devices, products and processes, including design and construction. It excludes routine testing and analysis of materials, components and processes, e.g., for the maintenance of national standards, as distinct from the development of new analytical techniques. It also excludes the development of teaching materials that do not embody original research.

---

1   Scholarship is defined for the RAE as the creation, development and maintenance of the intellectual infrastructure of subjects and disciplines, in forms such as dictionaries, scholarly editions, catalogues and contributions to major research databases.

Funded Research is not for Everyone

Not everyone needs or wants research funding. Although most academics regard part of their jobs as including both research and teaching, the research component of their job description is, for many, adequate as it is. At the barest minimum, it means keeping current in their field; for many it is a requirement of their institution that they are engaged in research as a condition of their employment.

A professor who is expected to spend, say, a third of his or her time on 'scholarship' may be able and willing to conduct that research relatively independently, perhaps only depending on a departmental secretary and research students for support and resource. Many people only need and prefer this arrangement. Once they move towards gaining research funding, several features of their work will change dramatically.

Changing the World

Jane Hunt, a contract researcher in the area of public consultation, is partly funded by Nirex (the UK body responsible for managing radioactive waste). She knows what it is like to be a contract researcher, and an academic who has needed to adjust to a different culture.

When I met Jane she was dressed comfortably and casually in jeans and a sweater – 'my work clothes' – and recalled feeling awkward the day she bought a suit before one of her important meetings. I asked if she felt then like she was 'playing the game'. Yes, she agreed, she did, but –

> I'm playing a bigger game. In the particular
> world I'm working in, they need some good
> ideas. It's a nudging process.

That means, for researchers like her, it is a matter of short-term adjustments to achieve long-term goals and strategy. This depends on relationships, not one-off, short-term projects. Those kinds of projects are more for consultants, not academic researchers. Jane is clear about the boundary between academic and consultant. A consultant, she explained, may simply do a 'literature search' in two days, write a report and be finished.

> The knowledge gained is then kept and sold:
> it's about the commodification of knowledge.
> I am not like a consultant. I am genuinely
> trying to change the world.

It may seem paradoxical that that is exactly why she is respected within Nirex. Jane's client, Communications and Decision Analyst Elizabeth Atherton, told me she likes to work with Jane because they share the same values: the importance of public consultation.

If Jane needs to buy a suit in order to 'play the game', it may be a small price to pay for changing the world.

Sometimes, the prospective partner may be unaware initially how the world needs changing. Thus began a long and mutually satisfying relationship between Unilever and the Centre for the Study of Environmental Change (CSEC) at Lancaster University.

The first collaborative project concerned genetically modified (GM) foods. At the time the initial research idea surfaced, in 1996, the idea of genetically modified foods had not swept onto the public agenda. That was precisely the reasons the group at Lancaster wanted to research it. Said a researcher involved on the project, Phil Macnaghten:

> We had some kind of cosy sort of idea of corporate responsibility but there's so much fluff going on that we needed something that was substantial and would actually galvanise people. We were thinking – we don't want this to be just some sort of corporate effort. We want this to actually be real, and we were very keen on this, so we chose the issue of genetically modified food. It was likely to lead to potential controversy, so the question was – let's do some public research on this issue to see the way in which the issue was being framed both within the regulatory world and the corporate world, and indeed the NGO world, to see how it panned out in relation to ordinary members of the public.

The CSEC framed their proposal around finding out how informed different sectors of the population were about GM foods and how they felt about the issue. As one of the world's largest consumer goods corporations, Unilever had logged the issue of GM foods on its corporate radar as an immediate and long-term concern.

The four-month research project consisted of nine discussion groups composed of people from a range of different gender, class, and socio-economic backgrounds. It included particular groups, such as a group of schoolchildren, and a group called 'risk takers' – people who like taking risk with their lives, engaging in such practices as drag car racing or other dangerous sports. The findings challenged and conflicted with Unilever's corporate policy at the time.

What the researchers found was that the more that people thought about the issue, the more concerned they became. The CSEC team were able to take the nature and implications of GM foods and situate them within the context of the sociology of knowledge. What appeared to be at stake for people was more complex and inter-related than previously expected. Their findings pointed to genetic modification of food crops to be closely bound up with trust and risk. Feelings about GM foods were seen to confront ethical boundaries about the integrity of life, leading to many unforeseen implications which may be irreversible.

As risk became the theme of the GM research, it also underpinned the research relationship itself. Looking back now, Phil remembers that feeling of risk:

> There was the risk for us to work with a
> corporate sector. What does that mean in
> terms of our integrity? The risk for Unilever
> was to support and publish a piece of
> research which was at the time diametrically
> opposed to the company's policy.

Six years later, the CSEC/Unilever relationship was still thriving and several more research projects had been successfully undertaken. How and why the relationship continues will be explored further in later chapters. While the specific goals between funder and researcher did not appear to be the same at the beginning, a more fundamental driver was recognised. Phil Macnaghten summarised the relationship this way:

> The reason we got involved with Unilever
> was a marriage of interests. It was really an
> early attempt to think about wider issues of
> corporate social responsibility.

What the relationship provides, according to the CSEC client at Unilever, is 'intellectual thinking'. Clarissa Hughes, Consumer Science Leader for the Laundry business, says that it gives a 'societal dimension to risk strategy, complementing other business dimensions', allowing the company to make better decisions.

Changing the world is not something that happens overnight, and not all research can be expected to affect immediately the decisions and actions of others. A major, five-year ESRC-funded programme: 'Children 5–16' is a good example. In his address at the programme's final conference[2] Programme Director and Stirling University Professor of Sociology, Alan Prout, told delegates that the programme's aims included:

> [to] make a significant contribution to knowledge of the changing conditions of childhood and children's everyday lives and to contribute to public policy debates about children's participation, interests, rights and responsibilities; and to examine children as clients and consumers of child services and those which implicate children.

But, I wondered, were there specific actions which he had hoped would result, and was he disappointed if they had not occurred? I put the question to him in later correspondence.

> I wouldn't say any policy change will come about because of research alone. This raises an interesting point about social science and policy. In general (there are exceptions no doubt) research rarely leads directly to policy change. I always saw the Children 5–16 Research Programme as contributing to a wider policy debate, involving many different constituencies and taking place over a long period. I thought the Programme should inform this debate and discussion rather than try to lead any particular changes.

Against the Odds

Public research money is not, according to many researchers, distributed fairly amongst institutions. Higher Education Institutions (HEIs) which score best on the UK's Research Assessment Exercise receive more funding than those who do not. Many people are critical of this approach, arguing that new universities or those without a record of accomplishment in research can never break through into the 'elite' arena.

2   www.hull.ac.uk/children5to16programme/conference.html

While the good news is that funding is increasing, the bad news for many is that it is not being distributed evenly. One-quarter of all research income from the HEFCE goes to just four universities – Oxford, Cambridge, University College, London and Imperial College, London. Those which have the highest research ratings receive more money leading, some argue, to an inevitable structural elitism in education. This would potentially disadvantage newer universities with less research record and less infrastructure to support it.

Professor Howard Green, Chair of the Modern Universities Research Group (MURG), believes that the dual support system affects research outcomes which in turn affect research funding. Due to the emphasis on the RAE, modern universities get very little from dual support. The kind of research most often done in the modern universities is different from 'traditional' academic research in that it is more practical, applied and professionally related. Much of it is funded by outside agencies, such as industry or local government, and due to restrictions on intellectual property, much of it does not get published in peer review journals. This means that much of the research activity in modern universities is at the edge of what the RAE defines as research. This affects the entire research process because academics have less time to create proposals for external funding. He says: 'This lies at the heart of institutional funding. It is the underlying reason that we must ultimately be systemically disadvantaged.'

Part of MURG's response to a HEFCE consultative document made that point precisely. It disagreed with the statement that the quality of research should continue to be the sole basis for assessment in the RAE, saying that 'the RAE process should recognise that different disciplines have different characteristics of excellence, and panels should be able to make their judgements drawing on evidence provided specifically for their discipline'. When, however, MURG nominated people to sit on the RAE panels, only eight of its 42 suggestions were accepted. At least, he stressed, that was eight more than before.

MURG also recommended that excellence in research is not just measured by how 'international' it is. Why should local or regional research not be excellent? It recommended to the HEFCE that its funding should encourage research of local, regional and national importance.

But all, in his view, is not negative – 'there is also a mythology around new universities, that we get a raw deal'. The situation is not quite so monochrome. A few years ago the ESPRC did a study on research funding and found that while the new universities were less successful in winning research funding than the older universities, the gap was not as big as might have been expected. This, he suggests, shows that the quality of applications from the modern universities is high.

The study also found that there were fewer applications from modern universities, reinforcing the systematic disadvantage theory and supporting the notion that if academics at modern universities had the same amount of time to work on proposals as their colleagues in the older sector, they would be able to submit as many proposals. Another finding from the ESPRC study was that the size of the grants which were awarded tended to be lower for the modern universities than the older. This may particularly reflect the greater infrastructure at older universities, which can support the kind of research which relies on it – most notable in science and engineering.

Gender Issues and Research

Also, research money is not, according to at least one recent study, distributed fairly amongst men and women. To apply for most research projects, the principal applicant must be a senior member of the academic staff. This requirement reveals a number of related issues, notably that of gender bias.

A recent study by the National Centre for Social Research, commissioned by the Wellcome Trust and six research councils, enquired into why men win research funding more often than women do. The summary report by the Wellcome Trust[3] said:

> The awarding of research grants is at the very heart of the academic system. As research funders we know how many applications we receive a year and how many of those applications are successful. We also know that, in the UK, once an application is received there is no evidence of gender discrimination – men and women have similar award rates and this observation is consistent across a range of funding organisations. Yet, in reaching this conclusion it became apparent that gender may be a determinant of grant application

---

3   www.wellcome.ac.uk/en/1/awtvispolwmnwhoexe.html

behaviour – women, in general, were
applying for fewer research grants than men.

The study concluded that there was, indeed, a gender bias, but not one in the funding agencies themselves. The gender bias in funding is rooted within the structure of academe itself. The Trust continued:

> The findings from the study indicate that many factors influence grant application behaviour. The survey results show that women were as successful as men in getting the grants they applied for, but were less likely to apply for grants because of their status in the institution and the support they received. The main influences on grant application behaviour were: seniority, employment status, tenure, type of institution, professional profile, institutional support, career breaks and family circumstances. Whilst many factors affect both men and women, some disproportionately deter women from making applications. For example, criteria designed by research funders to help define who can apply for research funding can produce a gender bias at the application stage, because more women than men are employed on fixed-term contracts and are at lower academic grades.

Women are still under-represented within the senior academic tiers. This, the study concluded, explains why more men apply than women do and why, consequently, men win most funding. Although it was outside the scope of that report, it may be reasonable to extrapolate that other people not represented in the senior echelons will, too, be under-represented in both applications and awards: people of colour, for example; people with disabilities, people from different socio-economic backgrounds.

For anyone who believes 'the personal is political', this may be one very good reason to apply for research funding. Recommendations from the report urged funding bodies to review their policies to widen the criteria for application. Women, and potentially others who see a structural bias in academe, are encouraged to make statements within their funding applications about their particular circumstances.

Conclusion

There are many good reasons to apply for research funding, and some good reasons not to. What is required is a particular mindset that recognises that the hard work and disappointments that characterise the struggle for funding are rewarded not by a single cheque but by a partnership. Extending the marriage metaphor introduced earlier, the marriage of interests should not merely be a marriage of convenience built mainly on material value. The most successful funding relationships prosper because each partner is genuinely interested in the other. The reason they stay together is not that they have to, but that they want to.

Hard work is expected on both sides. It is hard work, but winning research funding is only the first step in a relationship which has risks and opportunities for both partners. Although it may appear that only the researcher makes the effort to accommodate different styles and expectations, the reality is different. Researchers influence the relationship and the funder.

For researchers, exerting that influence may be a matter of political as well as personal ambition. The current status quo does not reflect the needs and circumstances of many who are systemically disadvantaged – new universities, emerging departments and disciplines, and individuals under-represented by virtue of their colour, gender, or disabilities. It is, therefore, important that such people apply for and win research funds. There is, to state this clearly, no discernible intended or even unintended bias against women, ethnic minorities or researchers from newer universities – just that many fewer applications are received than from white males from established universities.

The game, undoubtedly, will change. It will change when funders receive more innovative and well-constructed applications from the systemically disadvantaged. In the meantime, for many people – like those whose work we visited above – they will play the game knowing that there is a bigger game at stake.

3 RESEARCH ISSUES

'What is this research about, and why is it important?' It seems like an obvious question but its neglect causes many research proposals to be rejected minutes after they arrive in the funder's office.

Any experienced research scholar will be familiar with the disciplines, processes and standards which must appear in an application. The research methodology must be robust, outcomes clear, time and money allocation appropriate, and so on. But these alone are not enough. If you cannot clearly and quickly communicate what the research is about and why it is important, your application may be read as unfocused and purposeless.

Potential funders need to be able to see, quickly and clearly, that yours is a partnership that can work. You must be clear about what the issues are. These are too easily taken for granted. It is important to take a step back and look at the funder's most basic critical issues.

Janet Lewis, former Research Director of the Joseph Rowntree Foundation, described her experience of research proposals which do not clearly state what they are about:

> There's the focus of the issue – does it fit into the priorities that we've identified? Have they addressed the issues? . . . the other thing is how people are proposing to do the work. I think the general standard of proposals has got better over the last few years, but we still get a lot that are under-specified in terms of method.

Those reasons affect applicants' success more than any other I discovered. Firstly, and most importantly, the researcher fails to articulate the issue. The reader finds it hard to get a clear picture as to what it is about or why it is important. Poor articulation of a problem or issue will often indicate to a funder a lack of organisational or communication ability, both of which are vital to successfully concluded research projects.

Secondly, the reader does know what it is about but the proposal does not fit funding priorities. The research proposal may be expertly written, the question well-framed and the methodology exquisitely designed. The outcomes may be clear, the time-scales and budget accurate and the references of researcher and research team impeccable. If the proposal does not, however, fit with the priorities and ethos of the funder in question, it will fail.

Table 3.1 is a good example of the clear guidance some funders give to prospective researchers.

Table 3.1 Joseph Rowntree Foundation Guidance Notes

What the Foundation does not support

With the exception of funds for particular projects in York and the surrounding area, the Foundation does not generally support:

- projects outside the topics within our Current Priorities;
- development projects which are not innovative;
- development projects from which no general lessons can be drawn;
- general appeals, for example, from national charities;
- core or revenue funding, including grants for buildings or equipment;
- conferences and other events, websites or publications unless they are linked with work which the Foundation is already supporting;
- grants to replace withdrawn or expired statutory funding, or to make up deficits already incurred;
- educational bursaries or sponsorship for individuals for research or further education and training courses;
- grants or sponsorship for individuals in need.

Source: www.jrf.org.uk/funding/overview/notsupported.htm

It is critical to note what is being said in Table 3.1. The Foundation is not making a judgement about the intrinsic worth of your proposal; it is simply stating its priorities and preferences. There will be funders, perhaps many of them, who will gladly underwrite your conference or fund your further study. The Joseph Rowntree Foundation is not one of them.

A successful funding application needs to address both those questions: how do you make sure you have the right fit between yourself and the prospective funder, and how do you know if that message is getting through?

Positioning the Issue

It has been said that if you cannot describe your view of the world, your religion or your philosophy in less than a minute, it is probably not worth saying. A weakness of many proposals is that the applicant had too general or vague a notion of the issue, or perhaps had a clear idea but failed to express it. Make sure you know the (short) answer to the questions:

- What is the research about?
- Why is it important?
- Who cares?

There are a number of possible ways to answer those questions. The research may, for example:

- add theoretically to the current body of knowledge through new thinking
- add empirically to the current body of knowledge through new evidence
- expose and correct an error which has been compounded over the years by researchers who failed to see it
- inform policy makers
- demonstrate a new way of applying the body of knowledge.

This does not presuppose that only one of those issues will be pertinent. Sometimes, they are interwoven and interdependent. The ESRC-funded Research Group on Families and Social Capital programme, based at South Bank University, is a good example. Here, issues of policy, practice and theory intertwine. Table 3.2 presents a summary of the issues.

Many people fail to articulate the issues because they have not made up their own minds about how far they can go in pursuing their research questions. What is the research really about and when will it end? No one can answer all the related questions about an issue and stay focused, but they can acknowledge that those questions exist while they concentrate on a particular aspect.

Once you sketch the boundaries, you can continue by acknowledging the related areas which you may not explore but which may be relevant. These can often be usefully cited by such phrases as 'While it is beyond the scope of this research to adequately cover ...' You, and your funder, will also know that research is a process of discovery and learning, and therefore new questions will arise during the process. The objective in this phase of your thinking is to identify the core issue upon which you will focus.

Table 3.2   Research Group on Families and Social Capital, South Bank University, London

The research group aims to:

- Investigate the relationship between family change and social capital in different circumstances and localities, taking a critical approach to the question of whether the dynamics of family and social change mean the death or generation of social capital;
- Explore these issues through three integrated strands of substantive work focussing on issues at the cutting edge of the dynamics of family change: ethnicity; education and employment; and intimacy;
- Develop theoretical understanding and empirical knowledge of the processes of the formation and sustenance of social capital for and within families by relating the strands of substantive work to three cross-cutting conceptual elements of social capital: identities and values; trust and reciprocity; and caring for and about;
- Refine understanding by moving iteratively between empirical data, conceptualisation, and engagement with research users;
- Adopt and develop appropriate quantitative and qualitative methodological tools to extensively and intensively investigate the generation of social capital within, and use of broad forms of social capital by, families and family members;
- Contribute to policy and practice in supporting families through providing accessible and informative strategic knowledge about the relationship between families and social capital.

Source: www. sbu.ac.uk/families

The ESRC's Global Environmental Change Programme is a good example. It was initially begun in 1991 to look at major global environmental issues such as climate change and biodiversity. As it evolved over the next few years, the research issues grew to include the implementation of sustainable development, at local, regional and national levels. The issue was therefore focused and yet sufficiently dynamic to allow growth and re-interpretation.

Why is it Important?

Why it is important will depend on who is asking the question. It may be important to you and your immediate colleagues, but to engage with a funder it has to be important to them as well.

For example, an ESRC-funded programme, The Future of Work, presented its main issue clearly and described why it mattered:[1]

> Few subjects could be judged more vital to
> current policy and academic debates than the
> prospects for work and employment. Will
> there be sufficient employment opportunities
> to support the aspirations and well-being of
> future generations? Will the jobs and
> workplaces of the future assume a radically
> different character? Are we poised to witness
> a radical re-drawing of established divisions
> between paid and unpaid work?

That would be too large a topic for one research team to cover. It took more than 100 leading researchers on 27 different research projects across the United Kingdom five years to explore that issue. Individual projects explored different aspects of the future of work, such as the future of unskilled work, the nature of home-working, the changing character of the employment relationship, business re-engineering, performance, the determinants and distribution of caring work, the scope, content and impact of human resource practices, the significance and diversity of temporary work, the employment patterns of Pakistani and Bangladeshi women, the different systems of care work for the elderly in five European countries, the role of trade unions in promoting employment opportunities for ethnic minority women, the implications of the forces of internationalisation for patterns and places of work, employer strategies, and the sources of conflict, cooperation and partnership at work.

All these diverse proposals were successfully submitted for funding by the ESRC. They were all able to identify, effectively, how they tackled one or more of the issues raised in the ESRC tender invitation and relate their substance to the 'vital' questions posed by the ESRC.

Who Cares?

If you were doing independent research, or research as part of your job, it may be enough to satisfy your needs and the needs of your employer: choose your focus, articulate the question and apply the usual processes of method and outcome. But once you make the decision to look for external funding,

---

1   www.leeds.ac.uk/esrcfutureofwork/synopsis/programme.html

something changes. Now, your research issue will not be important to you alone, or to something we might abstract as 'the body of knowledge'. To consider external funding you will need to know how the research issue matters to the funder. You are, effectively, being sponsored for your research. Who cares about the same issues you do?

This turns the question around now, from simply focusing on what we want to do as researchers, and what the funder wants us to do. Maintaining the principles of partnership introduced in the last chapter, it is evident that their interests and our interests should converge.

This may be hard work. Many academics find it difficult to turn from the conventional approach related above, where the research issue emerges from an area of interest, to an approach where another party's interest has to be given at least equal weighting. Professor David Crowther, head of research at London Metropolitan University, is candid about it:

> The hardest thing I always find is to structure
> a bid in a way that enables me to do the things
> that interest me, and meet the needs of the
> organisation who's providing the funding.
> That is, it is crucial to phrase the bid in an
> appropriate way for that organisation. I find
> that quite a difficult thing to do.

It is not surprising that it is difficult. It is not the way we are trained to think as academic researchers, where the field itself or the research we have recently done provokes questions which are worthwhile in their own right. The difference when we seek funding is that we need to find other people who share our feelings of worth. What do they value? What do they care about?

Responding to the 'Wrong' Issues

A common route to funding is to respond to a call for tender, where an organisation may advertise or otherwise circulate a call for tender. At this stage the problems have already been defined, as have the questions and therefore often the method.

The academic may immediately sense a problem, familiar to researchers: is it the right problem? Are those the right questions? Are they approaching this the right way? To an academic with a deep understanding of the area in question, it may be evident that the answer is 'no'.

How do you respond to something that is misframed? Broadly, you have three choices:

1 Say it's a stupid project and refuse to respond. This will ensure that you do not waste your time or tarnish your reputation by involving yourself in work that does not meet your academic standards. It will also mean that any potential of influencing the funder is abandoned.
2 Respond with a hint, saying something like 'The topic is very important but it may be fruitful to look at it from a different angle'.
3 Run with what they ask for but know at the outset that one of your findings will be that the question wasn't right.

The most constructive step is the second. Although there appears to be a certainty and finality in project objectives, many funders will consider your points of view. The Joseph Rowntree Foundation, for example, is willing to negotiate on particulars but only once the project is funded. This means that you need to enter with a spirit of trust and collaboration so that they will see that you are sufficiently aligned with their ethos to be able to work out the details and direction. The empathy with which you frame your proposal will communicate this.

Although the third point may seem tempting, most funders will see through it. They are not interested in a half-hearted piece of work which ends with an 'I-told-you-so' insult. If you are interested in a relationship rather than a one-off transaction, this is not likely to be a satisfying route.

Ideally, you will find yourselves in the position of 'favoured supplier'. This is when you are known to the organisation. You will be approached even before the call is circulated and will be asked for input at the stage before the question is formed.

Empathising with the Funder

Which comes first: the call for tender or the call to funder? While most researchers respond to calls for tender, there are some who favour a more proactive approach. These researchers do not wait for contracts to be posted; they seek and follow opportunities. If, like Jane Hunt, they are interested in increasing transparency and public consultation within the environmental sphere, proactivity will be the most effective route. After all, if an organisation is inclined to insularity and secrecy it will not be splashing out on advertising for external help. In Jane's case, she wanted to know why Nirex, a leader in the industry, did not even have a website. What did that say about its attitudes towards openness and public consultation? Having identified the issue of public consultation, it was not long before Jane was working with Nirex on projects to improve their transparency.

Their current website[2] shows that they have taken great pains to step away from their previous insularity. It covers what the organisation does, its history, all of its annual reports, and even details of recent board meetings. This would not, arguably, have happened without the commitment of a researcher who wanted to influence the area which most concerned her: the nuclear industry. Taking the initiative to seek and then win research funding from Nirex was not just a matter of paying a few bills; it was a challenge to transform industry practices. Proactivity, it seems, may be a question not just of pragmatism but of principle. And yet, those principles need to be communicated empathetically, in a way that seeks common ground rather than confrontation.

Returning to the earlier example of the Joseph Rowntree Foundation, what they care about is firmly embedded in their history and ethos. How many prospective applicants take the time to read that history and empathise with its implications? The Foundation grew out of the Joseph Rowntree Village Trust which was set up by Joseph Rowntree in 1904. He was concerned about housing and other conditions that people were living in as a result of poverty. The three trusts he established were to explore and respond not just to material conditions but their root causes. In particular, he cautioned researchers not to focus on 'superficial manifestations'.

Since then, the themes have evolved but they retain their focus on change. Issues of interest will therefore be those which can lead to policy changes and other actions. Other funders may not put the emphasis on change and action, but the Joseph Rowntree Foundation does. Researchers only interested in writing for academic audiences need not apply. How the funder values research will derive both from its history and its future.

Together with any funder's themes and ethos, any researcher will be guided by ethical guidelines which govern research within any particular discipline. The guidelines normally cover all the issues presented above and can be accessed through your individual department or professional association.

---

2   www.nirex.co.uk

Conclusion

Undertaking funded research is a different proposition to the undertaking of independent research. With no external third party to satisfy, research topics and issues can emerge organically from the data gathered, or be framed around the researcher's own interests.

Funded research means that you are often responding specifically to a funding proposition which is clearly specified. Funders – charitable trusts, research councils, professional bodies, companies or others – normally feel the need to set clear specifications as they are committed, often quite passionately, to achieving some specific type of change and progress.

Even when submitting a proposal in a responsive mode, the funder will have strategic aims for specific schemes and overall long-term strategies and objectives. These need to be studied and met.

This is not research 'in the abstract', with a view to adding to the body of extant knowledge. More than that, it is adding to the community of researchers and scholars in a given area. However well-planned, well-framed and well-presented a proposal might be, however robust the methodology, however interesting, many funders will not support research proposals which do not fulfil their stated aims. A very simple, very effective activity a researcher can undertake is, therefore, to study as thoroughly as possible all available information on strategies, themes, priorities and aims, noting any areas which are particularly encouraged and any areas which are normally precluded.

Don't presume that an evaluation panel will be able to conclude independently that you have understood the needs of the funding body. Reflect those needs back, explicitly. You want your reader to see that you have understood their stated priorities, and this is how you, the researcher, are addressing them.

Funded research is normally about the process of matching your interests, competencies and track record as a researcher with the needs of the funding organisation.

In making this match, and in meeting the explicit (and, sometimes, implicit) needs of a funder, it is important to communicate an understanding of these needs, as clearly as possible. In a research summary or abstract, say *who* (the research affects), *what* (the research is about), *where* and *when* (it will take place), *why* (it is important), and *how* (it will be approached).

- If you understand the needs of the funder, reflect those back explicitly to the funder in the proposal.
- If you do not, you are not yet ready to submit a proposal. Do more research and reading until you do.
- Try to understand and appreciate any underlying ethos, values or vision of a funding body.
- If you are clear about who, what, where, when, how and why, state that, clearly and simply.
- If you are not clear on who, what, where, when, how and why, you are not yet ready to submit a proposal.

In the next chapter we look more closely at the point of the research. What are its implications? What are the outputs. In other words: so what?

4 OUTCOMES AND OUTPUTS

What is an Outcome and an Output?

Many researchers find it difficult to step back and look at their work from a neutral perspective. Why is the issue important and to whom? This is the great 'so what?' question that needs to be answered in simple, clear terms. What will happen because of your work? Why should anyone, including yourself, invest time and money in researching it? Just as we explored in the previous chapter, the answer to that question will depend on whom we are asking.

A body such as the British Academy, for example, may agree that research into eighteenth-century lyric prose in Antigua is a worthy project and will enhance future research. Adding to the body of knowledge, pushing into new areas of thinking, finding little-known artefacts and analysing them, creating an archive or a dictionary – all these are important, have value to someone and fall into the remit of the British Academy. Another funder might not find the outcomes of any interest. This entirely relates to *their* values, ethos and priorities. It does not say anything about the intrinsic value of your work.

That is why we look at outcomes and outputs. Outcomes and outputs are the specified, or intended, 'so what?' benefits of funded research. A funding body will, depending on their values, issues and ethos, specify or intend that certain things should happen as a *result* of research being done. The outcome for a student researcher studying for a higher-level degree will often be a personal one: he or she will develop the skills to be a more adept researcher. Funded research goes a long way beyond the development of personal skills and knowledge, although of course it does deliver that. More on this theme is explored in Chapter 12.

There will, in all cases, be the need to show results which directly impact in a positive way on the mission or ethos of the funding agency and correspond to the ethos of your discipline.

But before we go any further, let's clarify exactly what we mean by *outputs* and *outcomes*. An *output* is what is tangibly presented to a client (in this case, a funding body or individual) during or at the conclusion of your research. An output is *put out* from your research. Every funded research project must have tangible outputs. These are often specified in precise terms (like the output of a Ph.D.: this many words written in this format, presented in this way, containing these specific sections). A specified output or outputs might be, for example:

- a book
- one or more learned journal papers
- a confidential report for the funder only
- a generally accessible summary posted on a website
- a 10 000 word report intended to be available in the public domain
- a TV series

or any combination of those and other outputs.

An *outcome* is something which is *expected to happen* as a result of the research being done, which is in line with the stated goals of the funding agency and the funded research. An outcome *comes out* as a result of your research. As such, it is normally much less certain than an output. Any competent researcher working to a brief can produce a specified output. But an outcome – something which happens as a result of your research – depends on others finding the work accessible, credible and valuable enough to use it. An outcome might be tangible (finding a chemical agent which allows particles to be held in suspension within a liquid, which means that an oral medicine will deliver its dosage more accurately) or much less tangible (contributing empirical data to a policy think tank on the future of work which will inform government thinking on city centre development and infrastructure long term). It may provoke change or inform policy in the wider world (research on child poverty, third world debt or global warming) or in a more bounded community (research on consumer choice amongst competing brands of toothpaste).

Finally, in terms of definitions, an output will often be asked to include a description of actual or intended outcomes. In some cases, part of the ongoing research will be to monitor outcomes, and present outputs which describe these. Most funding bodies, all accountable in some way or other, take the idea of 'so what?' very seriously indeed, and so make sure that the recipients of funding answer the question carefully and clearly.

Stating the implications of your research is the moment when you crystallise the value of your work. This can be a disconcerting experience, for here you are setting out in black and white what you believe should happen as a result of the work you will do. Wouldn't it be easier to let them draw their own conclusions? Easier, perhaps, but only in the short term. A proposal lacking clear outcome implications will usually be rejected.

In the competitive world of research funding, the funder must see clearly why your research is worth its investment over the hundreds of others they could choose. Unless you are able to demonstrate why it is important and what will happen as a result, they can too easily move on to the next application. You may show a grasp of the research problem, proper research design, and so on, all of which are important, but are considered as only the entry point for a good proposal. You need to move further: it is not the funder's job to try to decode what your significant value may be.

Even having warmed to the idea of your research, the funder will still want to know what you will do with the results. Is this simply going to be a private pleasure, in which case it will not be available to others? Should the funder invest in your genius alone? It is likely that they will not, and that if they did, other researchers might rightly object. Where is the body of knowledge situated? Not, surely, in your head alone. Other people who count themselves as members of an academic community believe that dissemination of knowledge is as important as its creation.

People who do not like the word 'output' or its commercial associations may take heart that it could be worse. The ESRC notes in making changes to its database of research outputs that the word 'product' could have been selected instead. A survey, however revealed that no one liked that term. The note explains that: 'People felt it suggested washing machines rather than academic endeavour! We've considered this carefully and decided to make the change and now use the word "outputs" to describe the wide range of items that can result from a piece of research.'

What is a Valuable Outcome and Output?

Value is decided partly by the researcher and partly by the funder. The value of the output is defined by those who have a stake in the outcome. That includes you, the funder, the people who will be affected by your research, your department, your colleagues. These and possibly others must be considered when you think through the value and nature of outcomes and outputs.

Due to the nature of general funding in the UK, what the Research

Assessment Exercise[1] thinks about outcomes and outputs is particularly important. The guidance notes explain that such definitions are deliberately broad:

> In principle any form of publicly available assessable output embodying the outcome of research, as defined for the RAE, may be cited. HEIs must have confidence that any output cited will be fully and properly assessed: panels may not regard any particular form of output as of greater or lesser quality than another *per se*. In addition to printed academic work, research outputs may include new materials, devices, images, products and buildings; intellectual property, whether in patents or other forms; performances, exhibits or events; and work published in non-print media. The only exception to the requirement that outputs must be publicly available is where they are confidential. Examples would include research reports for companies that are commercially sensitive, or reports for government departments or agencies that have not been released into the public domain. In such instances, institutions will have to make appropriate arrangements for panels to have access to the outputs. Responsibility will rest with the submitting institution to ensure that all necessary permissions for access to confidential work have been obtained.

This implies that private sector funding in itself will not prevent assessment by the RAE, but rather whether researchers choose to submit those outputs. The RAE is also not entirely wedded to traditional academic peer review systems. This more flexible approach may encourage less established researchers or those whose research is valued by the funder differently than journal editors or reviewers value it. The key is to be able to demonstrate that there has been an assessment:

---

1   www.rae.ac.uk

> Evidence that research outputs have already
> been reviewed or refereed by peers may be
> used by panels as one measure of quality.
> However, the absence of such review may
> not, in itself, be taken to imply lower quality.
> Panels will also have regard to all reviewing
> processes, as appropriate, including those
> operated *by users of research in commissioning
> or funding research work.* (emphasis mine)

This means that outputs of some funded research by organisations such as the Joseph Rowntree Foundation or the private sector can be included in RAE submissions. For many researchers this will make the difference between whether they strive for such contracts or not.

Notes within the RAE guidance documents specifically encourage a wide range of submissions:

> The Panel expects to receive and consider the
> following types of research output: papers,
> books and electronic material (e.g. CD-
> ROMs, videos, internet sites etc.). The Panel
> collectively will examine in detail virtually all
> of the works cited for all submissions. Where
> cited works fall outside the expertise of the
> Panel members other experts will be
> employed as specialist advisers or advice will
> be sought from other panels.

> All cited works will be judged on academic
> merit regardless of the medium or location of
> publication. The Panel will look for evidence
> of the following in judging the quality of the
> work cited: originality, contribution to the
> advancement of knowledge and
> understanding, scope or range of the work
> and scholarly rigour.

Different Partners, Different Outputs

Phil Macnaghten from the Centre for the Study of Environmental Change at

Lancaster University (CSEC), admits that the traditional attitudes have worked against him with regard to his work with Unilever:

> There are certain things which have been difficult. I mean, their [Unilever's] focus on high level quality reports has been fine but they haven't really been recognised sufficiently by the formal RAE processes. They don't have the same status because they don't come out of journals, they don't come out of peer review processes. And so, the translation of our work into standard journals has suffered.

That may be an unacceptable consequence for some researchers, but it depends on the motive behind the research. If it falls into the 'changing the world' category, it may not seem such a hardship. Phil elaborates:

> Our focus has been on change and working on real world issues of interacting and not so much on writing peer reviewed journal articles.

> I don't think you disseminate through journals, that's the point. Very few people read journals. Our report (for Unilever on genetically modified foods) has had a print run of around 3000 copies. This is double more than most academic books, and it has penetrated down into quality processes and into scientific processes. It has had an effect.

His client, Clarissa Hughes, agrees that impact is the most desired outcome. External publication may well be restricted due to commercial sensitivity. 'It depends on the project,' she explains. 'The closer to the business, the least likely it is that it will be published.'

Janet Lewis, former Research Director for the Joseph Rowntree Foundation, knows what she wants to see as an output: academic papers with minimal distribution are not on the list. This relates back to the ethos and history of the Foundation where action and change are the top priorities. She emphasises:

> Change doesn't happen as a result of the
> written word, change happens through
> people talking to each other.

The Foundation's policy on dissemination is particular and, in Janet's view, unique: 'I think we are completely unusual as a funder in our line on dissemination. I don't think anybody has actually taken responsibility in the way that we have.' As the Foundation is the largest non-research council source of social science funding, it will be worth our while to find out exactly what makes the Foundation different.

The Foundation's attitude towards outputs is succinctly summarised in how it frames the information.[2] Issues about dissemination and outputs are contained within a section headed: 'How the Foundation informs policy and practice'. This reflects its orientation towards outputs as drivers of change. As it states in the same document, 'The Foundation supports research and development projects in order to improve policies and practices either directly or indirectly.' Anyone applying for funding should therefore explain how their work will relate to policies and practices.

The two prime outputs researchers are expected to produce are a short, 2 000-word briefing paper summarising the project's main findings and a 15 000–20 000-word full 'accessible' report. So committed are they to the notion of accessibility, the Foundation provides guidance notes on exactly how to produce a report that is accessible. For example, the text must be well-structured, jargon-free and reflect what the project found out. Janet explains further:

> These reports are not the traditional research
> report, they are essentially writing the story of
> the project. We are really interested in
> producing research reports that are accessible
> to all kinds of people, so we want people to
> write it in a way that is likely to be interesting
> to people and to capture the essence of what
> they've found.

Recognising that it is usually difficult to find a publisher for a 20 000-word report, the Foundation has created a network of publishers committed to publishing its work. It also 'ring-fences' £5 000 of a project's budget to devote to dissemination.

This is an example of the relationship orientation the Foundation takes to its work. Researchers are expected to maintain the momentum after the project ends, taking an active role in dissemination. Apart from the contractual obligations entailed in the earmarked £5 000 funds, they are encouraged to submit academic papers and attend conferences if they so wish, understanding that, as its guidance notes state: 'the Foundation welcomes this activity and recognises its value, but does not regard purely academic outputs as a priority for its funding.' It goes on to stress that while it appreciated the value of peer-reviewed books and journal articles, it does not see them as a priority. That does not mean that researchers working with the Foundation will be deprived of time or money to produce the more traditional academic outputs. The Foundation admits it is 'sympathetic to requests for modest amounts of time for staff on short-term contracts to write for learned journals etc. after our priorities have been met.'

Those two examples, one from the private sector and one from a charitable foundation, illustrate how important it is to learn what a specific funder considers a valuable output. The ESRC, for example, defines outputs as the results of research and may include books, conferences, articles, databases and broadcasts. What remains the single theme for them is the availability of the output. The ESRC maintains a database with public access to the research they fund.[3] The Regard database contains summary details of all ESRC-funded research since 1985 and helpful links to sites and organisations related to ESRC Centres and programmes.

An interesting feature of the Regard database is its dynamic approach to outputs. Researchers enter their research abstracts once the contract is awarded, they update their entry as the research develops to report any changes, they offer links to their project's website if they have one, and they submit a final report of the research and its outputs when the research ends. They are encouraged to update the database as new outputs develop.

The AHRB may appear not to be so concerned about outputs in its definition of research by stating in its guidance notes[4] that 'research is primarily concerned with research processes, rather than outcomes' but presumes that something, nonetheless, will happen as a result of their funding:

> It must define a series of research questions
> that will be addressed, or problems that will
> be explored, in the course of the research. It
> must define its objectives in terms of

---

3 www.regard.ac.uk
4 www.arhb.ac.uk

> answering those questions, or reporting on
> the results of the research.
>
> It must specify a research context for these
> questions or problems and explain why they
> need to be answered or explored; what other
> research has been, or is being undertaken in
> this field; and what particular contribution
> this specific research project will make to the
> advancement of knowledge, understanding
> and insights in this area.

The research application should therefore explain why and how knowledge
will be advanced. In particular, the AHRB is concerned with developing
individual scholars. As part of its mission statement says, the AHRB:

> support the development of highly qualified
> people in the arts and humanities, both to
> supply the next generation of scholars and
> more generally to enable students to achieve a
> high level of knowledge, understanding, skills
> and competences that will be employed in a
> wide range of professions and vocations.

This is why they stress that applicants should say why doing the research is
important to them personally and how it will affect their career. Or, in other
words, how can your career path be seen as an outcome of this research
activity?

It is important to think through the number of outcomes and outputs you
may have, and the number of groups which might benefit. There may be
more than one beneficiary of any research project. Mohamed Zairi, Director
of the European Centre for Total Quality Management at Bradford Business
School, believes he delivers outputs and outcomes in three major ways. His
first concern is to deliver to those he describes as his 'primary stakeholders',
his funders. Secondly, he delivers internally to the university, 'because the
investment for us is not the money. The money is just a means to an end.'
What the university gains of more importance is expertise, by either
strengthening the existing expertise or adding in new areas of expertise.
Thirdly, it is publication:

> I think as far as practically possible, we try to
> publish all the research projects that we do. It
> would be a sin not to. At the very least we

would write up the project for our teaching.
The best thing we can do is serialise in a good
journal the design of the research, the data,
and the findings. That's three or four papers
right there.

Another example of multiple outcomes and outputs is the ESRC programme,
Children 5–16, which made a point to include the 'subjects' of the research as
beneficiaries of the outputs. This means, in terms of accessibility, outputs
need to appeal to five-year-olds as well as fifty-year-olds. As their website[5]
describes:

Forms of dissemination will include: targeted
seminars, briefing papers, accessible
publications, also directed at children, as well
as traditional academic output, national and
international seminars, working papers,
refereed journal articles, and books.

Conclusion

The themes running through this chapter stress three main points. Firstly,
every funded research project must have tangible *outputs*, be that a book,
a journal paper, a confidential report for the funder only, a generally
accessible summary posted on a website, or any combination of those. If not,
it will not be seen as a valuable exercise to the funder or, indeed, to the
researcher.

Secondly, most funded research will in one way or another, lead to an
outcome. That is to say, something will be expected to happen as a result of
the research being done, which is in line with the stated goals of the funding
agency.

There is no such thing as the right or most valuable outcome or output. The
value of the outcome will relate to the values of the funder and the
researchers. Some research projects are never funded because the funder and
the researcher have different ideas about what outputs were important and
cannot reach a consensus.

Thirdly, researchers need to find out which funders will be the most
appropriate for them in terms of valued outputs and outcomes, and address

5   www.hull.ac.uk/children5to16programme

the proposal accordingly. A useful site for assessing the major funders is the Higher Education and Research Opportunities website.[6]

In the competitive world of research funding, the funder must see clearly why your research is worth its investment over the hundreds of others they could choose. Unless you are able to demonstrate why it is important and what will happen as a result, they can too easily move on to the next application. You may show a grasp of the research problem, proper research design, and so on, all of which are important but are considered as only the entry point for a good proposal. You need to move further: it is not the funder's job to try to decode what your significant value may be.

In looking at outputs and outcomes, think about stakeholders in the research. These will normally include:

- Funders – what Mohamed Zairi at Bradford Business School called his 'Primary Stakeholders'
- Your university/department/centre – what is the university gaining in expertise, experience and reputation?
- Researchers themselves – often through public domain exposure of their work through publication, conferences and the like. In some cases, a number of papers can be derived, for example, on the design of the research, the data, and the findings.
- Those affected by research outcomes – who will your work be helping? How will that look?

---

6 www.hero.ac.uk

5 WHAT IS GOOD RESEARCH?

This book would not have been written had there not been a growing pressure to seek research funding. This is a time of diminishing public funding and mixed attitudes towards public support for universities and research. The trend, undoubtedly, is towards gaining funding from other sources.

Some people are increasingly concerned that this trend will affect the quality of research. Before we move on to the techniques of gaining and maintaining research relationships, we might consider the qualities that people mean when they think of 'good research'. This chapter summarises the key points of a separate but related study undertaken specifically on the question of what is good research.

People may define 'good' and 'research' differently, but when I interviewed a number of researchers and students about the question, I encountered a surprisingly high level of consensus[1] which matched funder's and assessors' notions of what is 'good'. The qualitative judgments were aligned and will be discussed in more detail below.

Another question I explored at the same time was how people used research. Were there differences between how, say, professors used research compared to students and might this therefore impinge on what they thought was 'good'? Is there a difference between how a researcher and funder uses research and will this therefore affect their judgements?

For an American Professor of Human Resource Management, good research is:

> Research which meets criteria of rigour, a
> systematic kind of modelling in its
> articulation and which ties back its process to
> a solid grounding in what we know about the
> area that is being researched, so that there is a

---

1 Interviews were conducted in mid-2000 with a US Professor of Human Resource Management, four British Professors in sociology/social sciences, and three Masters students in the same field. Their comments are multi-level, as originators, evaluators and consumers of research.

total integration of varying viewpoints in the
grounding of the research design. Then in my
mind for it to be good, it must then be very
focused.

Good research is also grounded in theory. One of the four British academics
interviewed described 'ideal' research:

For me, the challenge is to do research that is
well-rooted in theoretical debates and
conceptual discussion. Research can only be
good if it stands on a firm footing. It has to be
clear about the concepts.

Another British academic reflected a similar theme, saying that empirical
disciplines must be tested empirically. While there are many possible
approaches, the right approach is determined by the research question.

In recent years we've seen develop a
multiplicity of research methods, surveys and
techniques to try to tease out meaning. Good
qualitative research is consistent with the
data, theoretically exciting, imaginative, and
convincing. It is able to extend or develop or
modify a theoretical notion that's around in a
literature.

Another British academic extends the concept of interdisciplinary and
imaginative research:

It's empirically based. It uses current ideas
and methods appropriately. It has a degree of
imagination and creative thinking. It engages
not only the person doing research, but those
reading it. My orientation is applied. It needs
to be accessible to all sorts of people . . . In my
personal opinion, it's important to be
interdisciplinary.

And in similar vein:

Good research allows the reader to re-
interpret the data. It rarely ends with an
answer . . . The writing up needs to show
transparency, honesty and recognition of the

limitations of what you did. The best research
is self-reflective.

An MA student's definition is similar:

> Good research would involve being part of
> the research situation. By that, I mean that
> research would not merely involve a god-like
> researcher applying his/her terms and
> categories to other people. Good research is
> dialogue.

The answers I found did not situate good research as purely objective,
standing outside the problem, trying to prove something. While good
research seeks evidence, it also seeks to *engage* people. It is accessible to all
sorts of people. The involvement of the reader, perhaps a reader who is not a
scholar, is part of what makes it good. The researcher is part of the research
itself.

As one British sociologist pointed out, that does not make it easy to evaluate
compared to standard quantitative research.

> Quantitative research may be easier to
> evaluate, because it makes fewer claims: it's
> hypothetical and then deductive: 'either you
> do it well, such as designing questionnaires
> properly, which is fairly straightforward, or
> you don't.'

Although that is a common perspective, people have developed methods to
evaluate qualitative research which is having an impact. That it is a common
perspective, however, bears thinking about when creating a funding proposal.
How will you help the assessor evaluate your research? How does your choice
of research method affect it?

The Funding Perspective

The Higher Education and Research Opportunities website[2] offers guidance
for new researchers and specifically addresses the importance of method:

> Good research practices are necessary if you
> are to produce professional and rigorous

---

2   www.hero.ac.uk

work. Attention to detail in your
methodologies and administration is vital for
your findings to be valid and make a real
contribution to your discipline. This can be
intimidating for new researchers, but there
are many resources available for reference
and help.

One problem in not getting the method right is that it often reveals a basic
misunderstanding of the issue or the problem. One funder remarked that
inattention to method is often a clue that the applicant does not understand
the funder's requirement; another funder said the problem may be one of
complacency amongst experienced researchers:

> The problems for social science is that we've
> got such a range of possible ways of doing
> things, that you need to be quite experienced
> to set up a good research design and also
> know what you're talking about when it
> comes to method. I think an awful lot of
> people who are in senior positions, who tend
> to be the ones who apply for grants, are
> getting lazy about this. They're resting on
> their laurels.

Finding the appropriate method will be even more complex if you are
applying to do a project within a larger programme. Here, you will need to
assess how your method ties in with other projects. Does it, in the words of
one programme director, show clear added-value to the programme?

Method and other factors affecting 'good research' will arise indirectly as well
as directly through funded projects. As we have explored already, the UK
Higher Education Funding Bodies use the results from the Research
Assessment Exercise (RAE) to help determine research funding (see Table
5.1).

Within its 'Unit of Assessments', it may embrace a wide spectrum of
approaches, from philosophical to applied. Its concern is 'research
excellence', defined by individuals on each panel. Its guidance notes
summarise this judgement thus:

> Panels will use their judgement in applying
> the descriptions attached to points on the
> rating scale. They will form a view on the

Table 5.1 RAE research definitions

The RAE defines research rather broadly, including work which contributes to the body of knowledge as well as that which contributes to commerce and industry. Their judgement about the quality of research varies according to levels:

5*   Quality that equates to attainable levels of international excellence in more than half of the research activity submitted and attainable levels of national excellence in the remainder;

5   Quality that equates to attainable levels of international excellence in up to half of the research activity submitted and to attainable levels of national excellence in virtually all of the remainder;

4   Quality that equates to attainable levels of national excellence in virtually all of the research activity submitted, showing some evidence of international excellence;

3a   Quality that equates to attainable levels of national excellence in over two thirds of the research activity submitted, possibly showing evidence of international excellence;

3b   Quality that equates to attainable levels of national excellence in more than half of the research activity submitted;

2   Quality that equates to attainable levels of national excellence in up to half of the research activity submitted;

1   Quality that equates to attainable levels of national excellence in none, or virtually none, of the research activity submitted.

Source: www.rae.ac.uk/Pubs/briefing/note9.htm

> quality of all the research activity presented in
> a submission in the round.

How, researchers may ask, will that view be formed? As with all assessments, it will be based on the opinion of the assessor. There is not one universal definition of good research: *what is good research is defined by those who assess it in particular instances.* The implication for researchers is, of course, to discover who the assessors are and how they reach their judgements.

How Research Gets Used

The usefulness of research depends on the role of the person and what he or she perceives that role to be. When teachers use research as examples for teaching, even 'bad' research can be 'good'.

Professional researchers based in institutions may 'use' research to increase their standing and therefore their likelihood of gaining funding. The student who wants to use the right research to please the right professor is doing much the same thing: both are seeking to increase a perception of their credibility and knowledge.

Good research thus satisfies the objectives of many different people and sectors. This does not in itself present an insurmountable problem where, say, the researcher is faced with conflicting objectives and definitions of what is good.

It was precisely that quality of multi-dimensional approaches to good research that was praised in a report on an ESRC-funded project led by Professor Rod Rhodes in the Department of Politics at the University of Newcastle. The programme, Whitehall, The Changing Nature of Central Government in Britain, ran between 1995 and 1999 and comprised 23 projects in two phases.[3] Its objectives were to create a better understanding of both recent and long-term changes in the nature of British government and how those compared with changes in similar governments in Europe. It also aimed to develop new theoretical perspectives and new research methods as well as encouraging interdisciplinary work and new researchers. A particular emphasis was put on dissemination.

It is therefore apparent that what was 'good' about that research project would depend on a variety of aspects. An excerpt from the final evaluation provides an excellent example of how 'good' the project was in the view of its assessors:

> The published research-based profiles of some key aspects of UK central government have been transformed by the Whitehall-programme's work; the large number of books and Rhodes-edited book chapters listed for 2000 or 2001 will provide the record. (Examples include the prime ministership; the governance of policy network based constellations of interests; and the formal regulation of government and extra-government processes). The Director's achievement in publishing alongside his grant-holder colleagues to the extent listed in the report is remarkable. Together with his

---

3   www.ncl.ac.uk/politics/resources/whitehall/

propagation of the Whitehall-programme
within and beyond this country, it has
provided much more than a mere
complement to the projects' own
achievements. Together, his work and theirs
has constituted an academic campaign of real
distinction, perhaps unique in British social
science to date. Advances in methods,
creating and lodging new data sets and
achieving some training among the projects'
junior researchers and associated PhD
students are all covered in this report. The
Council and the civil service have had an
excellent return on their investment in the
Whitehall-programme and its extension
projects, both from the projects and the
outstanding quality of the Programme's
direction.

'Good' may be linked to subjective, qualitative statements which vary not
only by person but by purpose. People evaluate and use research differently.

Good research uses appropriate methods, and in its writing up the author
makes the process transparent. Many examples of published research are not
transparent. The 'sample' I interviewed was small and cannot be generalised
to the academic or student population as a whole, but it raised some
interesting questions and insights which may deserve further research.

The main implication I would draw is that no method is value-free and
therefore the scholar must not only become aware of his or her values but also
make them transparent to, in this case, the reader. This brings a different
meaning to the word 'good' and how we might define ethical research.

Secondly, issues identified for further research are usually, by their nature,
difficult to research. When looking at a call or considering responding to a
funder's theme, it is useful to bear this in mind. If they knew the answer, they
wouldn't be asking. Research is something we do when we don't know the
answer.

Some areas for research may lie outside the experience and understanding we
have as a body of researchers. We need to guard against protecting only those
research areas which match our skills and backgrounds. Although we
necessarily need to present ourselves as credible researchers capable of

completing the assignment well, it is unlikely we can do it alone. We will need complementary skills to expand on our own.

Another implication concerns the mask we choose to wear. If we are to learn more about implicit beliefs, about meaning in different cultures and languages, then we need to have more than 'right' methods to do it; we need humility. This may be determined less by our theoretical knowledge as sociologists and more by how we listen and generate discussion. It is how British sociologist Beverley Skeggs began her research with working-class women:

> I knew little about methodology and began
> the research by just hanging around and
> talking to the women as much as possible
> (Skeggs, 1997, p.22).

It gets right to the heart of how we see our roles as researchers, funders, teachers and students.

Conclusion

There is no single definition of good research. Good research is defined by those who assess it in particular situations and circumstances. When working to the needs of a funding body it is useful to find out as much as possible about the assessors.

However, 'good' is not purely situational. In looking at some of the terms used across various research councils and funding bodies, and the university research supervisors and professors I interviewed, some themes emerged.

The word *interdisciplinary* (or cross-disciplinary, or multi-disciplinary) was used several times; the idea was that research might be stronger if people brought skills and knowledge learned from one discipline to bear on an adjacent area. The notion of the research teams, and how they might be selected and managed, will be discussed later.

Whether discussing large or small-scale research, empirical or ethnographic, detailed data analysis or, as Beverley Skeggs put it, 'just hanging around and talking ... as much as possible', most people I spoke to used the term *rigorous*. Whatever the approach, it must not be sloppy; it must be thoroughly thought through, without loose ends. Funders typically are trying to deliver outputs based on strongly-held beliefs and values, and proposals must demonstrate attention to detail.

All funded research will have some kind of clear and visible output, and for that reason, another important term used is *accessibility*. Beyond publication in a highly specialised learned journal, research funding bodies need usually to demonstrate to their own funders, or trustees, that money has been well spent. This may involve the sharing of some or all of the written research output, and being able to say, clearly: this is what we did; this is how it will benefit people.

An interesting term also much used was *transparency*. In other words, be clear about your limitations; be clear about your own interests and background. Don't bluff your clients. No research methods are value-free; the more transparent you are in discussing them, the closer to 'good' your research is likely to be.

Finally, when I conducted this particular research exercise I was surprised that so little is known about the criteria funding bodies use for rating research. The implication is that a lot of time and money could be wasted. In the next chapter, we will look at value, costs and the research budget.

6 THE VALUE OF RESEARCH

What is it Worth?

How much can you ask for? How much can you get? How much do you need? These are questions people frequently ask when they think about winning research funding. By phrasing the question slightly differently, however, the researcher can create a more realistic and usually more productive approach. It is not always the best option to try the low-cost route in the (mistaken) belief that this will make the project more appealing. Low cost often equals low value.

If you think about your own life, this may ring true. There is a certain price you expect to pay for quality. Organically grown strawberries cost more than the intensively grown variety. Most of us would be somewhat alarmed to be offered a new BMW at the same price as a used Escort. What's wrong with it, we wonder? And yet, too often we do not place the same value distinctions on our own work.

How much is the research worth? To undervalue your own research sends a negative message to the prospective funder. Suppose, as is quite likely, that the person reading your proposal is an expert in your field. Perhaps this person has conducted similar research. She knows it takes at least six months to collect the source material you need, and another three to analyse it. How do you think she will react when you claim you can do the whole job in half the time? What are you – a speed reader, some kind of savant, or just someone who has not really thought through the task which lies ahead? Someone, she may conclude, with insufficient respect for the enormity of the task and its significance: someone, in short, without respect for the field and for people like her.

The previous chapters have discussed what your research is, why it is important and to whom it may matter. These are the first steps in forming a sense of the value of your research. Underestimating the value may demonstrate not only a lack of confidence but an indication that you may not be capable of conducting the research. If you have not allocated sufficient time and resources to the project, how sure will your funder be that you can complete it?

One research project was nearly rejected by a funding body precisely because of that reason, as one of its directors explains:

> One of the referees recommended against acceptance because it appeared we had over-estimated our ability to complete the project in 18 months. We reviewed that feedback and agreed we had not devoted enough time to it, considering what we wanted to do. We expanded the project to two years, asked for fifteen thousand pounds more and got it.

Less is, therefore, not necessarily better. Funding organisations do not reject research proposals because they cost money. Spending money is not an unfortunate but unavoidable side effect of a funding organisation's work: spending money is their work; it is what they do.

Remember, the day a funding organisation has an unspent budget is one of their last days in existence. They justify their existence by giving you money. When they do so, they are not doing you a favour: they are fulfilling their objectives. The ESRC is straightforward about it in its guidance notes,[1] saying that every year it invests more than £48 million in 'funding the highest quality research and developing the resources that underpin the UK's social science base'.

Note that the largest funder of social science research in the UK does not give money away. It invests money. Its language is one of 'funding investments' which it makes available primarily through its Research Grants, Research Fellowships, Research Programmes and research centres. In its guidance notes the ESRC is, again, pointedly stressing investment rather than cost. It states that the four characteristics of all successful ESRC research applications are that they not only 'promise excellent research', nor are they just 'of value to potential users outside or within the research community', nor that they convince the reviewers of the researchers' ability to conduct the research properly, but that they can 'demonstrate value for money (not necessarily the same as cheapness)'.

How does this translate into practice? The British Academy, for example, is clear and practically focused about how to provide value, even when attending conferences. Many academics find conferences a refreshing opportunity to renew acquaintances and form new ones, to 'network' and share ideas about research. To qualify for BA conference funding, however,

---

1   www.esrc.ac.uk

the academic needs to demonstrate value for money. Its guidance notes[2] include a statement of what value is. Assessors look for:

> academic merit taking into account the scholarly standing of the proposed conference in the international field, its likely impact upon the subject area, the focus of the conference programme and theme(s), the importance of having British participation in the conference, the scholarly standing of and contribution to be made by the named speakers (if named), presentation and intended outcomes. Assessors may also pay attention to issues such as the projected spread of attendance, and value for money.

It is also clear about the assumed value of pilot projects, which it views as 'pump-priming' to allow the viability of potential research to be explored before applying to another organisation, such as the Arts and Humanities Research Board or the ESRC for the larger project. And yet, even pilot projects which do not go forward must demonstrate a value, as the Academy states in its guidance notes: 'Wherever possible, the pilot project should be framed so as to indicate that some worthwhile outcome will result, within a fixed time span, even if the more substantial research project does not succeed in attracting funding'.

Other funding organisations are likely to be equally concerned about the value for money. The Arts and Humanities Research Board, for example, was established in October 1998 to provide support for research in the arts and humanities, just as the other more established research councils support the sciences and social sciences. One of its strategic aims in its corporate plan[3] articulates this objective:

Strategic Aim 7: SECURING VALUE

> To ensure the best possible use of public funds by ensuring value for money and demonstrable value in all the Board's programmes and activities.

Here, the AHRB explicitly links its work to creating a return on the

2   www.britac.ac.uk
3   www.ahrb.ac.uk

investment from public funds. The Board accepts that defining and monitoring such an aim is difficult, but it still must be pursued:

> The peer review process on which the Board depends for allocating funds in order to sustain and raise the quality of the activities in which it is involved employs a variety of criteria, depending on the object of the particular programme and scheme. Assessing the comparative value of different kinds of funding and different kinds of award is by many seen as difficult either in terms of academic or other criteria. It is critical to the Board's effectiveness that it should none the less be able to reassure itself and those who fund it of the value for money that its funding represents. A determined and defensible approach to this task will be a prime aim of the Board.

Even more clearly, the plan ties this broad aim to specific objectives:

> <u>Objectives</u>
>
> The Board seeks:
> to include in all its assessment procedures a mechanism for explicitly identifying and recognising value for money
>
> to include in all its monitoring activities a mechanism for testing value for money in scrutinising the value of its own funding to ensure that external assessments and judgements are taken into account.

With that objective in mind, it should naturally fall upon the prospective researcher to ask: 'how am I helping?' Is your proposal and, in particular, your budget supporting that objective or making it more difficult to attain?

Value to your Community

The idea of adding value to the academic community strongly influences a funder's view of your worth. Steve Morgan, Head of Corporate Projects and

Evaluation with the AHRB, stresses the importance of articulating how your research affects your research community:

> We look at the vitality and vibrancy of the
> community as a whole. The way in which we
> get to that value is to fund individual
> activities, with the individual seen as part of
> the community.

The researcher may look at it the work purely from an individual or a team's point of view, whereas the AHRB must look at the researcher as a member in a community. To be of value to the AHRB and its communities, the research must reflect the aims of the specific scheme within which an award is being sought, as well as the wider strategic aims of the AHRB. Ultimately, that means it needs to be of value to the people to whom the AHRB answers. Steve explains: 'Funding agencies have a higher paymaster to answer to – a government department, and through them the Treasury and eventually parliament.'

How is an individual researcher to know how parliament, and eventually the public, defines value? That is not too difficult, Steve points out, if the researcher reads the aims and objectives. For example, a researcher applying for Research Leave can see that one of the stated aims of the scheme is to enhance the researcher's ability to finish a piece of work, which would lead to dissemination. This links back to the strategic plan's aim of encouraging dissemination. The strategic plan is produced following government consultation which in turn suggests that it is a priority in the UK for publicly-funded works to be made accessible to the public. Steve advises:

> A common problem is that researchers focus
> on their own particular area and see
> themselves as a world leader in their field.
> That may be true, they may be a world
> leader, but they need to understand that we
> will receive applications from 300 other world
> leaders. It's a matter of mapping to reflect the
> strategic value of that research to the board.

The pressure for researchers to demonstrate the value of their work is felt everywhere in the research community. The comments of Sir Howard Newby, Chief Executive of the Higher Education Funding Council for England, in December 2002[4] are instructive:

---

4   www.hefce.ac.uk

Universities and colleges are to be congratulated for this outstanding performance. The outcome of the 2001 RAE demonstrates the value of awarding research funds selectively to reward quality. The improvements in performance since the last RAE are a direct result of institutions managing their research strategically. They have used their funding selectively to build their research strengths in a very impressive and cost effective way . . . Research is a major driver of productivity, quality of life and international competitiveness. It is vital that we secure the necessary resources to continue to build on the UK's leading position in international research.

So far in this chapter, the emphasis has been on understanding value in the widest sense, particularly the concept that funding agencies invest in researchers. Eventually, this idea of value must be translated into actual numbers, but the more time spent considering how value is created, the better. As Steve Morgan of the AHRB observed: 'The application forms are carefully constructed so that you first need to think through what it is you want to do, and then work out how much money you will need to deliver that.'

Striking the Budget

When preparing the budget, most university-based researchers will receive help from their own finance department and, particularly, their research support unit. In most cases, the only items which can be funded are those which are exclusively devoted to the research itself. These are known as 'direct costs'.

Direct costs are those which, in the words of the ESRC, 'can be uniquely and unambiguously identified with a particular research project'. The implication here is that costs must not only be properly connected to the project, but they must be seen to be so. In other words, expressing in vague terms that miscellaneous expenditure is required will not be acceptable; saying that ten car journeys at 34 pence a mile are planned is an unambiguous and acceptable statement.

Generally, research funding covers:

- travel and subsistence
- research staff hired for the project – either by salary or daily rate
- fieldwork and surveys carried out by third parties
- consultancy payments
- specialist software
- equipment used directly and exclusively for the project (usually assumed to have a shelf life of three years or a portion of the final payment may be deducted for its use after)
- direct office expenses such as postage and telephone.

Most funding organisations, with a few exceptions, will not normally pay such expenses as:

- employment of established academic staff (Research assistants hired specifically for the project are allowable, but costs of established, full-time members of academic staff are not)
- general overheads such as heating, lighting, central computing costs, insurance, security, cleaning
- building construction, maintenance, renovation, rent, leases
- hospitality or entertainment
- general travel for the purposes of general study
- books normally obtainable from the library
- consultancy payments within the institutions of applicants or co-applicants
- contingencies or miscellaneous expenditure
- dissemination expenses, such as copying and printing unless specifically agreed.

When it comes to how to cost the project, again the ESRC stresses value and investment, not cheapness. Its recommendations for applicants in its guidance notes[5] include:

- Justify your costings, which should be considered with care and close reference to the ESRC Research Funding guidance.
- Be realistic – lavish costings are unlikely to find favour with the Board and a proposal which promises the earth at remarkably low expense will be regarded with caution.
- Think carefully about the time and resources needed to complete the research successfully within the specified period.
- A well thought out financial plan helps to create confidence in the proposal generally. Give as detailed a breakdown of costs as possible so that the Board can properly assess the case for support.

---

5   www.esrc.ac.uk/ESRCContent/researchfunding/

- Do make sure that what you are asking for is allowed within the regulations.
- Bear in mind that the Board is looking for value for money.

Otherwise, the proposal will fail, says the ESRC unequivocally: 'Unrealistic costings, unconvincing management plans, and a host of other factors will also play a part in the downfall of many proposals.'

It is a time-consuming but important task to go through all the notes available on what an organisation does and does not fund. Just finding the appropriate category may be difficult until you familiarise yourself with the particular funder and how the logic works. If you are considering applying to the British Academy for travel expenses, for example, there are several options. If the proposed travel is linked to a UK research programme, for example, you can apply under Small Research Grants or Larger Research Grants. If the travel is linked to a research programme abroad, you can apply under those two schemes or to the International Activities programme. If, however, the travel is for a conference, you should look to the Overseas Conference Grants or International Collaborative Programmes. Just sorting out the options can take more time than many academics can afford.

The Research Administrator

Research administrators can help in many ways. The most important aspect of the research administrator's role is to guide applicants through the sometimes messy maze of terminology and techniques involved in creating and monitoring a budget. Their professionalism in their work increases all the time. Their professional network, RAGNET, provides training and a support network for administrators to exchange best practice and to raise the profile of research administration as a profession. Their website[6] is worth a visit to see the breadth of programmes and events designed to make them better at their jobs – and the life of researchers that much easier.

Many academics are unaware of the significant amount of work these administrators do on their behalf and how they can work better together. Applications for funding need to go through the university's research support offices. The research staff can help, in particular, with the budget. They will advise and check on all costs, in particular ensuring that staff costs are in line with established daily rates, for contractors or consultants, and with university scales for employees. Given their experience, they will know better

---

6   www.ragnet.ac.uk

than most applicants will how different funding agencies work and what their requirements may be. They can also advise on contracts and other issues, such as intellectual property rights.

Research administrators also know the differences between public and private organisations and how they budget and cost items. There are, for example, differences in how they allocate overheads and differences in how costs are expressed and monitored, whether by the project, the day or the hour.

Conclusion

While different funders may have different systems and different ways of costing research, their common theme is value for money. In this chapter, we have looked at how that value can be best expressed in terms of contributing to the wider academic community and the funder's objectives.

Bear in mind the ESRC guidelines that successful research proposals:

● promise excellent research
● promise research of value to potential users outside or within the research community
● convince the reviewers of the researchers' ability to conduct the research properly
● demonstrate value for money

Demonstrating value isn't about preparing a low-cost proposal any more than it would be about preparing a high-cost proposal. It is about understanding the needs of the research body and showing, clearly, how value is being added by what you propose.

The study of a funder's notes for guidance, which are normally quite explicit, is therefore an important piece of preparation.

The person who may be in the best position to help frame a proposal in terms of value for money is a research administrator. Look at the Research Administrators Group website,[7] to get a feel for the job of the research administrator. Make sure you are allowing plenty of time for your research administrator to make a useful input to your budgeting.

---

7   www.ragnet.ac.uk

7 TEAMS AND NETWORKS

Many new researchers are surprised that the success of their project will not depend so much on their personal skills and intelligence but by how well they work with other people. In this chapter, we look at teams and networks to illustrate the nature of collaboration from the smallest project-based unit, to university inter-departmental groups, to networks drawn from different regions or countries.

Even small research projects involve other people to some extent. A historian working on an archive project, a classicist doing an international exchange, or four people from different European universities collaborating on policy issues, all need 'people skills'.

In its guidance notes, the AHRB emphasises people skills as well as traditional research skills such as data gathering and analysis. In its section titled Networking and Teamworking, its says that students should to be able to:

- develop and maintain cooperative networks and working relationships with supervisors, colleagues and peers, within the institution and the wider research community
- understand one's behaviours and impact on others when working in and contributing to the success of formal and informal teams
- listen, give and receive feedback and respond perceptively to others.

It is therefore apparent that the ability to work well with other people is noted as a key skill. This becomes particularly apparent with larger projects which are often complex multi-disciplinary, multi-institution, multi-country entities. For European Union funding, which is multi-institution and multi-country, people without previous team management experience will be expected to accept a junior role in any prospective team. Only those with a previous international track record in leading multi-institution teams may consider themselves for the position of coordinator.

Collaborating in teams will be essential for new researchers, to enable them to be guided while gaining experience. This has become a particular issue for the newer universities which may yet not have acquired a research infrastructure.

Professor Howard Green, Chair of the Modern Universities Research Group (MURG) stressed that 'When you have limited resources, focus and team work is especially important.' So are all methods of collaboration – collaboration with people within the university, in other universities, in other countries. Collaborative efforts can partly remedy financial hardships by sharing expensive resources such as scientific equipment or libraries.

Managing Research Teams

There is always a risk that a research team may fail to reach its goals due to a number of team-related issues. These may include differing expectations, role definition, and communication. In her experience as a researcher and team leader, Linda Woodhead at Lancaster University says that a common cause of project failure is that the team breaks down. This is usually, in her view, through lack of supervision. Too often, the team leader fails to lead by meeting the team regularly, and helping resolve issues and challenges as they arise. In this chapter, we explore how some people have resolved those issues and work together, successfully, often for many years.

Academics who lead research will find that they are sometimes simultaneously handling a number of projects varying in size and complexity. Professor Mohamed Zairi, Director of the European Centre for Total Quality Management at Bradford University, finds that building a strong team around him is the critical success factor. Building the infrastructure is essential, he says, because professors work on many projects, not just one. He says he thinks people skills are more important than anything else: 'You lead research, you don't do research.'

As a professor, he says, 'you develop a following. Professors are nothing if they don't have followers. The followers could be research students, could be associates, could be fellow academics working in partnerships and collaborations.'

The disadvantage, for many research team leaders, is that they cannot both conduct research and lead research effectively.

What Does a Leader Do?

One of the most difficult adjustments for research leaders to make is to distance themselves from the immediate research process. Leading a team means letting go of the day-to-day business of research – the literature reviews, the interviews, the detailed data analysis. The team leader's role is both one of project and intellectual leadership.

From a project management viewpoint, the job appears quite technical. There are overall strategic goals, aims and objectives. These are broken into discrete areas of work with timetables and milestones. The team leader is there to see not only that the separate parts of the project are proceeding to schedule and plan, but to anticipate and negotiate changes when those become necessary. Most importantly, the leader sees that the discrete parts work together in balance to contribute to the whole. Only a team leader with a helicopter-view of the whole project will be able to see how the parts fit and move together. Doing that essential task is what removes the role of team leader from that of hands-on researcher.

Professor Rosalind Edwards at South Bank University, who is currently directing a five-year ESRC-funded programme on Families and Social Capital, says that is one of the hardest parts of her job. Directing a team of professors and researchers is vital to the success of the project, and she is the first to admit that it is interesting, invigorating and challenging. Leading the first ESRC programme at a new university is an enormous responsibility and privilege, she says.

> But I often feel uneasy when I listen to the
> other researchers in the team meetings talk
> about their work. Part of me wants to be
> doing the interviews myself, to be interpreting
> that data.

Further, as a well-published feminist of some note and authority, she can gain some satisfaction in at least the partial realisation of a political goal to see more women in senior positions of both structure and power. Realising that goal is satisfying, but is not without its disappointments. When she created the team for the ESRC proposal she knew she had to make tough decisions about who would belong and who would not belong. This contravened some of her feminist ethics about inclusivity, but was necessary to create a balanced team.

How does the team leader create an effective team and help the members work together well? This captures the essence of collaboration, something most people will say they want and like, but many find difficult in practice. Janet Lewis, former Research Director of the Joseph Rowntree Foundation, observed that effective collaboration is something missing from many research teams. Lack of leadership is, she agrees, often a factor in project failure but just as important is lack of true collaboration:

> I think some of the problems arise from the competitiveness in universities now. This is often reflected in research proposals which are not really seen as collaborative kind of endeavours.

On large programmes, the concept of collaboration extends beyond the immediate project team to the programme as a whole. The themes and outputs can be spread across different projects as well as focusing on the overall programme. The ESRC's Democracy and Participation Programme, for example, was thought to be urgently necessary in light of the government anticipating significantly greater citizen participation in the future. It included collaboration between disciplines as diverse as politics, sociology, social policy, geography and education and promised to 'provide new conceptual thinking about the nature of democracy and representation in a technologically advanced and rapidly changing society'. Outputs ranged from papers to conferences across the breadth of the programme.

Seeking and maintaining a constructive collaborative environment becomes the focus for many successful team leaders. It influences from the outset how the team is constructed.

Professor David Crowther, Research Director at London Metropolitan University, says his goal in creating effective teams is to demonstrate that the team members have different areas of expertise that complement each other. He not only constructs the team that way but stresses in the proposal the complementarity of the different experiences of the people involved. His initial step is to talk to one or two of the people who have expressed a common interest in the subject and from there consider who else would add value to that team:

> It always starts off with an interest in the topic area – the requirement of the bid will bring more people in. When I talk about teams I'm talking about a minimum of two and a maximum of five people. You go above five – it starts to get hard to co-ordinate, especially when you're talking about people from different institutions.

There may be other reasons beyond expertise which influences team creation. Janet Lewis gave an interesting example of how the Joseph Rowntree Foundation responded to inclusivity issues and 'emancipatory research' in research proposals.

> There's a disability movement who are rather
> committed to saying only disabled people can
> do research on disability, which we don't buy,
> but there is certainly something that we do
> buy, which is that the research agendas
> should be set by the people who are affected
> by the project, not by researchers. We believe
> there should be a partnership arrangement
> and in some cases we have wanted to
> encourage disabled people to put in
> proposals, even though they aren't really
> researchers. We're concerned to try to
> support people who are wanting to do
> interesting work, to help them to do it.

In that case, the team would need to include not only a disabled person but somebody more experienced in research. Another example she gave was that of a junior researcher who submitted a proposal but the assessors argued against approving it because she had no track record in research. Rather than simply reject it, they worked with her to find a senior academic to support her. In that case of a junior researcher, Janet's belief is that it's sometimes necessary 'to try to provide the back up and support that they need in order to be able to achieve what they want to do'.

The role of a team leader will include:

- Targeting the appropriate funder or responding to a request for a proposal
- Researching the suitability of the funder before submitting a proposal
- Selecting the appropriate team
- Creating the budget
- Writing the proposal
- Meeting the potential funder and making presentations when appropriate
- Finalising the agreement
- Working with the team to set schedules
- Meeting regularly with team members to explore progress
- Leading academic debates within the group to maintain intellectual rigour
- Ensuring the project adheres to budget
- Negotiating changes when necessary with the team and funder
- Reporting to the funder when appropriate
- Creating the final report and participating in feedback mechanisms
- Helping the team reflect on its learning.

Team Types

There is much interest in management research and practice in psychological approaches to team working, based on the idea that different people have different team preferences. Some, for example, might be more comfortable organising and leading, while others may prefer a support role. Widely used in industry and the public sector, the approach has yet to be used in depth in many universities.

Asked about the applicability of this approach, one research team leader commented:

> I haven't got to that stage yet and I think the reason is that environments such as the academic environment are not open to novel ways of motivating people. They expect academics to be motivated all the time. They're probably not.

The concept is developed from Carl Jung's work on psychological types (see, in particular, Jung, 1938). Jung explored different attributes of the extravert and introvert personalities and how they respond to poles of thinking/feeling, sensing/intuiting, and perceiving/judging. The extraverted nature, Jung argued, places an emphasis on finding meaning through external conditions rather than searching for absolute values within oneself. The introvert will maintain an abstracting attitude to the object whereas the extravert will be positively oriented:

> I need only point to the peculiarity of the extravert which constantly urges him to spend and propagate himself in every way, and on the other to the tendency of the introvert to defend himself against external claims, to conserve himself from any expenditure of energy directly related to the object, thus consolidating for himself the most secure and impregnable position (Jung, p. 414).

What Jung examined further was the implication of the broad extravert or introvert types in relation to how they think or feel, sense or intuit, perceive or judge. This may convert to behaviours often noticed in research teams, where some members may appear to ramble incoherently for several minutes before receiving feedback from others which subsequently helps them refine or reframe their thinking. This need to think aloud is typical extravert behaviour, quite distinct from an introvert's tendency not to comment or contribute to a discussion until thinking has become more certain and crystallised.

It will also influence how somebody creates and maintains formal and informal networks: 'What the one brings about by a multiplicity of relations the other gains by monopoly' (ibid., p. 415).

For example, the need for external information and validation can become extreme in those Jung described as extravert-intuitive types who become almost addicted to new possibilities and change, where 'stable conditions have an air of impending suffocation' (ibid., p. 464). This may be a recognisable type in many research teams – the one who tends to divert from the main question, who tries to invent or reinvent new questions and to resist coming to conclusions or defining outputs.

In terms of applying these concepts to real-life teams, the ideal situation following this analysis would be to combine people of both complementary and opposing types. One method used widely in many organisations is the Myers-Briggs™ instrument used in organisations by approximately 2 000 000 people a year. Though such instruments are open to critical evaluation, the point here should not be lost: any team is composed of real people with real personalities and predilections. It would be naïve to suggest that a research team is different or somehow above such dynamics. Whatever approach a team may use to explore its internal dynamics will normally benefit the way they work together.

Wider Collaborative Networks

From a small research project team we can look wider, firstly across the institution as a whole. Who else would researchers count as members of their collaborative networks?

One such group is the university-based research management and administrative team. Peter Townsend, a Research Manager in the Research Office at Loughborough University, says that the university has adopted a 'one-stop shop' from pre-award, to post-award. He says this is their preferred model to previous arrangements where the functions were split. By bringing pre-award and post-award together, at the same time co-located with external relations, intellectual property and the consultancy company, a 'corporate front door' has been created.

He is also secretary to the Research Committee which takes a university-wide view, defining research targets, allocating resources and helping the university manage its strengths and weaknesses in research quality and quantity.

One of the roles of his office is to target and disseminate funding opportunities to academics, which often means being able to identify the experts in the organisation. They use databases and networks to see what is being sought by various external bodies, and actively feed this information to academics.

He stresses the importance of not becoming too reliant on any one particular funder – government or otherwise. Research diversity leads to having a 'balanced portfolio', which is, in his view, a feature of 'healthy research'. Healthy research leads to 'healthy teaching' which, of course, sparks more questions and themes for more research.

One aspect of applied work is that it is often multi-disciplinary. This means that a researcher's collaborative skills are refined while knowledge is being stretched. An increasingly proactive element of his office's work is to encourage interdisciplinary and inter-institution collaboration, as reflected for example by the Engineering and Physical Sciences Research Council's (EPSRC) Basic Technology Programme.

The calibre of research managers and administrators is high and increasing rapidly, primarily due to the efforts of its professional association, the Research Administrators Group. RAGnet is a national network of some 400 Research Administrators which exists to provide training for Research Administrators, to provide a network for mutual support and the exchange of best practice and to raise the profile of research administration as a profession.

How can academics work with research administrators in their efforts to submit winning applications? A common response to that question was 'Involve us earlier!' It is far from unusual, I was told, for an academic to come to the support office in the morning with a funding application which has to be in the post later that same day. It would be a help if things were not always last-minute, although administrators are often quick to point out that organisation and micro-planning techniques are not attributes normally associated with academics: 'they just don't seem to think that way!'

If the application is successful, the research administrators will work to set up systems to administer the grant, working closely with personnel and payroll departments as well as the researchers. People will be paid on time, invoices sent at appropriate intervals to the funding agency and the final reports submitted.

What can the researchers do to help the administrators keep the project running smoothly? It may help to realise that a support office will have hundreds of grants running at any one time, with often only a few members of staff to administer them. The last thing they want are surprises.

The administrators I spoke to were all keen to be kept involved. Changes might occur during the course of a project and it helps to keep the administrators informed. Sometimes, for example, researchers might apply for an extension and forget to tell the administrator, or decide to spend more or less time on particular phases of the project which may have implications for allocations.

Finally, consider the widest possible networks. The will include your own discipline's association, as well as interdisciplinary groups, such as the Researchers' Forum based in the UK's Office of Science and Technology.[1]

Conclusion

The evident ability to work well with others is a key skill sought by many funders of research. This is because, in anything other than small-scale projects, research is a collaborative effort – collaboration amongst a research team, collaboration with the 'client' team at the funding institution, and possibly collaboration across different disciplines or institutions.

Research teams do not just succeed through the momentum of a project, or through the individual brilliance of their members. A good team needs skilled leadership to manage a range of issues from motivation to work division to deadline adherence to reflection on learning from the project.

Many businesses – but few universities – use psychometric profile instruments to help select 'balanced' teams. Probably the best-known and most widely used of these instruments is the Myers-Briggs Type Indicator™, MBTI, based on the personality theories and research of Carl Jung. The MBTI and other psychometric profile instruments help identify areas of work preference, which can give insights into how people can work effectively together.

---

1 www.researchersforum.gov.uk

Teams can also work on some research projects across disciplines and from different institutions. The same principles of team working and team leadership will apply but are likely to be even more in demand.

It is often worth involving research administrators in helping build networks for collaborative research.

PART *II*

IDENTIFYING YOUR RESEARCH PARTNER

8 THE BENEFITS OF RESEARCH PARTNERSHIPS

As we considered earlier, the benefits of research partnerships are greater than something as tangible as money, or even something more abstract, like security. Researchers and their funders who enjoy relationships based on the idea of partnership say most often that the greatest benefit is the opportunity to keep developing, growing and learning.

Universities UK, formerly the Committee of Vice-Chancellors and Principals (CVCP), takes the idea of partnership seriously. In its strategic plan: 'Vision, mission and goals 2001–2004',[1] it explicitly states that it expects 'Partnerships with a diverse range of private funders to continue to flourish and increase in number'. While competition both nationally and internationally will undoubtedly increase amongst universities, this also means that there are 'more opportunities for collaboration and strategic partnerships both within the UK and internationally'.

What do those partnerships actually look like, and why have them? Here, and in the following chapters, we can listen to some of those who think partnership is the right way to look at research funding. It is, however, not a model for everyone, requiring a different attitude to that which many academics might expect. There are compromises and disappointments, highs and lows. In short, like any relationship, funding partnerships are dynamic, unique and best conducted in an atmosphere of openness and trust.

Do you Want to Work Differently?

The essence of research partnerships is working together. This may mean shifting from an individual mindset to a team one. This will mean working with, for example:

- at least two, sometimes more, project supervisors at your own institution
- a team at your own institution within your own discipline or department
- an interdisciplinary/departmental team at your own institution

- a team including people from other institutions
- a team including a representative from the funder or an advisory council
- a team reporting into a wider programme, consisting of other projects within your discipline
- a team reporting into a multi-disciplinary programme, consisting of other projects from other disciplines
- a team reporting into a programme consisting of people from other countries, within or outside your discipline.

These are some, but not all of the possible configurations of the working relationships. Rather than see this as a drawback, many researchers want to engage actively in those ways and say that this is one of the prime reasons they seek such funding. This changes the emphasis from the 'expert' individual working, perhaps, with a helper, to someone working collaboratively.

It will be more likely that a larger team is engaged on empirical research than theoretical. Social Science is predominantly an empirical field, which demands external data collection. Researchers often work collaboratively across departments and with other organisations. Therefore, the model is 'team' rather than 'expert individual plus helper'.

The team approach not only applies to salaried academics, of course. The large and widening pool of contract researchers increases the need for collaborative approaches. By definition, contract researchers need to work with others. Along with the structural barriers facing contract researchers are the problems of loneliness and insularity. Toiling away alone for hours on a computer may satisfy a certain instinct for isolation, but most researchers find they benefit from exchanging ideas and the occasional joke or two.

The researchers and funders I spoke to described funded research projects in very specific terms. They are clear about what is required. In some cases, these might be foreign or awkward for some people in academia. For example:

- **Transparency:** The funder will want methods and costs detailed before awarding funding: some people are wary of being so prescriptive at such an early stage.

- **Accountability:** The structure of many research projects involve advisory councils or other people to whom the researcher must regularly report; this level of perceived 'supervision' is anathema to many research scholars.

- **Collaboration:** Small grants are available to individuals for conferences or one-off expenses such as building a database, but larger research funds demand a team effort. This is contrary to the solitary life some researchers prefer.

- **Culture differences:** Some funding bodies are organisations outside the academic mainstream. They will talk differently, think differently and have different expectations. They will normally expect the researcher to fit in with their ways, not the other way around.

- **Negotiation:** Some proposals require amendments from the funder. This process of negotiation can be an affront to what many people see as their scholarly independence.

- **Shared credit:** The team approach demanded by larger-scale research projects mean that members share results, sometimes diluting an individual's reputation as the prime expert in a given field.

- **Timescales:** In their quest for value for money, many public and private funders stress time efficiency. For many researchers, that translates as 'short-termism' and they worry that quality and rigour will suffer.

- **Multiple outcomes:** While research academics generally assume they will write an academic paper following a research project, some funders require more and varied outcomes, from reports to presentations. This demands different approaches and skills unfamiliar to many academics. 'I needed to use PowerPoint, not old-fashioned overheads, for presentations to the corporate sector,' said one researcher. 'I needed to figure it out by myself because no one in the department had a clue.'

- **Intellectual property ownership:** Who 'owns' the research process and findings is a thorny question for many researchers. Some funding relationships require significant shifts in the way researchers perceive their intellectual property. Some funders demand complete ownership of processes and findings. Some want co-authored papers, others are willing to let researchers take the credit.

What does a partnership actually look like? The relationship can be seen differently at different levels.

The Formal, Contractual Partnership

At a minimum, research funders will have some kind of agreement with the researcher. This is designed to ensure that money promised from the funder is delivered at agreed stages, and that the work the researcher promises to do will actually get done. It may set out other requirements, such as specific deliverables, and conditions, such as ownership of intellectual property.

Depending on the nature of the award, these requirements may be negotiable. The Joseph Rowntree Foundation, for example, is open to negotiation but only after the award has been granted. This reflects their belief that relationships based on trust and collaboration, where both parties operate with the same ethos, can always be worked out. It is a good principle for researchers to keep in mind when working with any funder: if the intention is to work constructively together, there should not be anything unpalatable in the contract. Why work with someone who imposes what you think are unreasonable conditions?

Another formality concerns 'branding policy'. Most funders expect award-holders to acknowledge the funder when they disseminate their research. Published papers, conferences, presentations and so on are all opportunities to keep the funder's name in the spotlight. This may seem of obvious importance to corporate funders who recognise the marketing benefit, but it is equally important to research councils or charities who want to position themselves in terms of their outputs. This is also a form of marketing in that it advertises the valuable work being done with public or charitable funds, and increases the likelihood of receiving more money in the future.

The branding policy may extend to naming a specific project, chair or building after the funder – the Saïd Business School at the University of Oxford, for example. Mohamed Zairi, Director of the European Centre for Total Quality Management at Bradford University, is known as the SABIC Professor after his sponsor, the Saudi Arabia Basic Industries Corporation.

The Learning Partnership

As one researcher put it, 'It's lonely in the dark'. One of the benefits of partnership is the knowledge that you are being supported as you venture into new and sometimes dangerous territories. The risk of failure may loom high for a researcher engaged in 'blue skies' research which has not been attempted before. Sometimes, a distant peer review process will not provide the working relationships necessary for researchers to feel sufficiently supported to take risks. Also, the peer review process means that there has to be an established field with experts in it who are able to evaluate your research. That presumes an orthodoxy in which some things are seen as legitimate while others are not. In a new field, finding the boundaries may be difficult.

Some funders pre-establish their research agenda through thematic priorities while others work more in responsive mode, where researchers set the themes and questions. These latter programmes offer wide scope for researchers to explore new or innovative areas. Some have such a wide scope that even the word *innovative* is not defined:

> The Innovation Awards scheme aims to support research focused on developing significant breakthroughs in knowledge and understanding, by challenging or radically extending existing models, perceptions, or research methods ... The AHRB has not defined 'innovation'. Applicants must explain how their research may shift or radically extend existing models. This could be determined in a variety of ways, from the way in which research is undertaken and the types of material investigated, to the interaction of different disciplines, techniques, or theoretical models, and the projected research outputs and ways in which they will be communicated.[2]

Not using well-tested research methods or even explaining what you mean by 'innovative' would be considered at the very least eccentric by most funding agencies and cause for immediate rejection by many. Only by engaging closely with a like-minded funder will a researcher be able to proceed into the unknown with any sense of confidence.

The desire to explore unfamiliar territory is shared by the funders as well as the researchers. Elizabeth Atherton, an analyst at Nirex who works closely with academics, explained that 'We needed to be at the cutting edge'. Her work is focused on making Nirex more open and transparent to the public, which involved new ways of thinking and working. In her experience, academics were able to 'push the boundaries' in a way which industry contractors would not.

'If you look at where the academic theory is compared to business and practice you will find a huge gap,' she says. A research partnership can help close that gap because both partners are willing to work with what they do not yet understand.

The benefits of this kind extend even beyond the principal investigator. Sometimes, other people in the department benefit by association. As Professor Mohamed Zairi says:

---

2   www.ahrb.ac.uk

My doctoral students often benefit from my relationship with our funders. Let's say they want to do a few case studies and they're studying something new, from a conceptual viewpoint. They might need a few initial, exploratory interviews. Because I have these partnerships, all I ever need to do is pick the phone up and say: one of my students is doing a doctoral programme on X, Y or Z; would you mind sparing a couple of hours and helping them out – and they do, time and time and time again.

Another example he gave was a global study on organisational values and their implication. It was a very difficult survey because they needed to penetrate into organisations, getting responses from top management, middle management, junior and people at the bottom. Some organisations distributed over 250 questionnaires for their workforce on his behalf: 'One hotel sent us 275 questionnaires back. The senior man himself was driving this, chasing people and saying – have you filled in that questionnaire?'

Partnerships can bring researchers new experiences and networks that directly help their research; they also indirectly help researchers and their institutions become better positioned for future work from other funders.

The Positioning Partnership

Partnerships offer unique ways to build reputation. For example, the AHRB actively encourages award-holders to remain involved with the Board. This may often occur through, for example, speaking at a seminar or leading a workshop on the agency's behalf. Or, sometimes external organisations need speakers and approach the agency for suggestions. The AHRB newsletter, *Arcady,* features researchers which helps build awareness of their particular work and the AHRB in general.

The ESRC database, Regard,[3] contains summary details of all ESRC-funded research since 1985. It also provides updates on research projects, showing how outputs have increased and researchers have continued to publish.

The ideal partnership is therefore one which allows learning on both sides, but there is still another benefit to be gained from that relationship. A

---

3   www.regard.ac.uk

working, enduring partnership will allow a researcher, or team or department, to build up expertise in one area. This can strengthen the position of the researcher (or department, or institution) to improve chances of winning future funding from other sources. Mohamed Zairi finds this one of the most valuable parts of his relationships:

> The meaning is the relationship. An organisation we know well, through other research, said to us here's ten [thousand pounds]: help us with benchmarking in the telecommunications industry. We've never worked in the telecommunications sector, although we know a lot about benchmarking. This was how we gained the knowledge and future credibility to do further work in that sector. This is not about money, it's about learning.

Another example was his work with an airline which had funded some of his earlier research. When he realised that to do further work in that industry he would need more detailed knowledge of airport facilities and cargo handling, he struck a deal with his client: he would be able to travel free around the network and examine their facilities in exchange for a report of his findings. As a result, the airline received specific insights into their operation while Mohamed gained necessary expertise in the industry which he could apply to future work.

The benefits of research partnerships are therefore both immediate and far-reaching. But, as with many partnerships, there is an exchange process: relationships will only work if both partners are prepared to give something back.

How can researchers ensure that the partner gains from the relationship in more ways than just receiving an end-of-research report? This reflects the nature of long-term relationships and how well the researcher can contribute to keeping the relationship mutually healthy. Some of their experiences will be more fully explored in later chapters when we focus on meeting expectations and maintaining the relationship.

Conclusion

The above points illustrate how differently academics may need to work when engaged in an externally-funded research project. In practice, many researchers find that the initial differences are neither deep nor systemic. It will be a period of adjustment and adaptation, even learning. It will be easier for most people to at least consider and be prepared for these adjustments at the beginning. Often, research proposals fail or projects founder during their infancy because the researcher has been unprepared for some of the new demands described above.

That is why it is so important that researchers investigate thoroughly the detail of a funder's style and expectations. Funding comes at a price. To some, it may seem like too high a price to pay.

Research partnerships, whether intra- or inter-institution, a collaboration with contract researchers, or an interdisciplinary or international mix of people, are increasingly an expected feature of a research proposal.

But the team is more than the group of people executing the research. To be really effective, the funder can be regarded as an active partner in the research, not just a passive client.

Partnerships usually contain three complementary elements; the contractual, the learning partnership and the positioning partnership:

- From a **contractual** point of view, a minimum requirement is that outputs are specified and timescales clearly drawn out, with payment schedules set against these.

- A **learning partnership** will mean that both parties may – with full knowledge and expectation – be outside their 'comfort zones' and exploring unfamiliar and innovative territory. A bold funding partner interested in a true learning partnership can be highly rewarding for a researcher.

- A **positioning partnership** will mean that both parties have an agenda, whether overt or covert, in terms of profile to be gained from the partnership. Normally, the more open all sides are about what they want to gain from a relationship, the more likely it is that a mutually satisfying result will occur.

9 PRIMARY FUNDERS

We live in a culture which espouses the importance of knowledge and learning. Most governments invest resources into the creation and management of knowledge, and into structures within which its constituents can learn.

But this investment is never completely open-ended. There are always limited resources at play, which means that some possible projects and programmes are supported, and some are not. Whenever public money is being spent on research, someone will be asking: is it fairly allocated? Is it being spent in the right areas? Is it too much? Is it too little? How, for example, do research councils, government departments and EU programmes balance the objectives of value for money and innovative research? Does it threaten or nurture the existence of a cooperative, collaborative academic community?

This kind of exploration is necessary to help refine a researcher's funding strategy. In this chapter, we focus on the two main funders of research in the UK: Research Councils and charities.

Competition for Funding

Public funding is increasing, but so is the competition for it. In March 2002, the Higher Education Funding Council for England[1] announced that its funding for 131 higher education institutions and 196 further education colleges will exceed £5 billion for the first time, representing a total increase of 6.8 per cent over 2001–02. Of this, £940 million would go for research, showing a 5.9 per cent increase. This includes an additional £30 million announced earlier in the year for departments rated with a 5* score.

Although the money is substantially more than previous years, it is still for some not enough. Sir Howard Newby, Chief Executive of the HEFCE, said:[2]

1   www.hefce.ac.uk
2   www.hefce.ac.uk/News/HEFCE/2002/GrantAnn.htm

> Although there has been an increase in
> funding for research, the total amount
> available is insufficient to fully fund the
> significant improvement in performance
> measured by the 2001 Research Assessment
> Exercise (RAE). We are committed to build
> on these excellent results – which
> demonstrate higher levels of world class
> research – and will continue to argue strongly
> for additional funding.

Along with this perception that more money is required generally, there is a
fear as discussed in Chapter 2 that new universities are not being fairly
treated by the system because they do not receive sufficiently high RAE
ratings to pay for infrastructure. This may make it more difficult for them to
receive awards from the funding councils or other bodies, partly because they
do not have the infrastructure to allow the time to create funding applications.
This, perhaps more than any other reason, makes it imperative that
researchers do not waste their time. They need to target and understand the
most appropriate bodies to create winning proposals and sustainable
relationships.

Given the range of funding opportunities, what influences a researcher to
choose the public sector as funder, and any particular public funding agency
as partner? Why would a researcher apply to the British Academy rather than
the Arts and Humanities Research Board? What attracts someone to
European Union funding and how is that difference from UK government
department funding?

Stepping outside of public money, what are the pros and cons of working
with charitable research trusts? Is there much difference between a charity
and a research council in terms of relationships?

Research Councils

Although there are differences within each research council, they all share
several common themes particular to public funders which must be well
understood by prospective research partners. Firstly, and most importantly,
public funders are publicly accountable and must therefore be sufficiently
transparent to satisfy their stakeholders that they are using public money
responsibly. Secondly, public bodies are staffed by civil servants whose
attitudes and ways of working will again be determined by the public

accountability and public service ethos. This means that direct relationships with individual beneficiaries of public money will be discouraged as they may suggest a conflict of interest.

These common themes present unique challenges and opportunities for researchers seeking the kind of funding relationship proposed in this book – one which is premised on familiarity, mutual need satisfaction and longevity.

Under the dual support system, the two major sources of public funding for higher education institutions in the UK are the Higher Education Funding Councils (HEFCs) and the UK Research Councils. The Research Councils were established under Royal Charter to fulfil the objectives set out by government in a 1993 White Paper called 'Realising our Potential'. Control of the councils is vested in the Department of Trade and Industry, supported by the Director-General of Research Councils, within the Office of Science and Technology.

The research councils are the largest funders of research projects in the UK, with the HEFCs providing background, infrastructure support. The Research Councils are:

- Biotechnology and Biological Sciences Research Council (BBSRC)
- Council for the Central Laboratory of the Research Councils (CCLRC)
- Engineering and Physical Sciences Research Council (EPSRC)
- Economic and Social Research Council (ESRC)
- Medical Research Council (MRC)
- Natural Environment Research Council (NERC)
- Particle Physics and Astronomy Research Council (PPARC)

At the time of writing in 2002, the Arts and Humanities Research Board (AHRB) was a charity, with future designation as a research council highly likely. The British Academy is an independent foundation.

The Haldane Principle

The independence of the councils is preserved by what is known as the Haldane Principle. This principle takes its name from Richard Burdon Haldane, Viscount Haldane of Cloan (1856–1928), described by the *Dictionary of National Biography* as a Scottish statesman, lawyer and philosopher. Politically, his sympathies were left of centre, first as a Liberal MP for East Lothian for 26 years and then as a Labour peer in opposition in the House of Lords. But it was his eye for organisation which most influenced

British government in the early twentieth century. As Secretary of State for War between 1905 and 1912, he reorganised the army; in 1917 he chaired a committee to reorganise government itself, which he found had suffered from haphazard growth.

Most significantly for those in education, Haldane was an early and vigorous champion of increased educational opportunities for people of all backgrounds, and dedicated much of his career to helping 'new' or what he called 'civic' universities developed in and outside London. He was one of the founders of the London School of Economics, a council member of University College, London, president of Birbeck College, Fellow and council member of the British Academy and eventually Chancellor of the University of Bristol from 1917 until his death in 1928.

In 1904 he chaired the government committee which recommended creating the Universities Grant Committee to advise government on how to allocate funds. In 1909 he chaired a Royal Commission on university education which reported in 1918. It was then that what we now call the 'Haldane Principle' emerged, namely, that research money derived from government sources would not be linked to government agendas.

The recent Quinquennial Review of the Research Councils (2001) reaffirmed the primacy of this principle, noting that successive governments have all endorsed the Haldane Principle as one of the prime protectors of the scientific integrity of research.

The nature of public accountability is therefore both subtler and more rigorous than it might initially seem. While on the one hand the government has no right to dictate what research is to be carried out using government money, it has the right and the obligation to see that public money is appropriately spent. This means that Research Councils must unfailingly report on how and why funds are allocated and demonstrate in sometimes painstaking detail that it is responsibly doing so. As long as this occurs, the Haldane Principle will no doubt maintain its influence, and researchers will enjoy a friendly distance from government. But it is also reasonable to expect that if successive generations of researchers and Research Councils fail to respect the obligation of public accountability, a less tolerant government may question the ethics of arm's length research which wastes precious resources.

Understanding this may provide insight for researchers who seek to form partnerships with those who receive government money. It can, perhaps, remove some of the frustration many people express about the detail, bureaucracy and seemingly onerous reporting and accountability methods used by the public sector.

Transparency

The drama and trauma of working with large organisations is thereby underpinned by the need for public accountability. The mechanism through which this is achieved is called transparency.

The Councils themselves are clear and overt about this responsibility. The Medical Research Council's opening statement on its web page tells readers that 'The Medical Research Council is a national organisation funded by the taxpayer'. The ESRC describes its new mission as emphasising that researchers 'engage as fully as possible with the users of research outcomes'. It even expressly tells researchers how to do that – by involving people from disparate areas from academe to businesses and voluntary organisations and by planning from the outset their dissemination strategy.

It is clear in its guidance notes that researchers should study their funding sources and understand the different missions. The ESRC, for example,[3]

> is an agency funded by the government and its mission is 'to promote and support by any means, high quality, basic, strategic and applied research and related postgraduate training in the social sciences; to advance knowledge and provide trained social scientists who meet the needs of users and beneficiaries, thereby contributing to the economic competitiveness of the UK, the effectiveness of public services and policy, and the quality of life; and, to provide advice on, and disseminate knowledge and promote public understanding of, the social sciences'.

Four characteristics of all successful ESRC research grants are constant. They must:

● promise excellent research
● be of value to potential users outside <u>or</u> within the research community
● convince of the ability to deliver research
● demonstrate value for money (not necessarily the same as cheapness).

---

3   www.esrc.ac.uk/esrccontent/esrcgen/displaygen/mission.asp

The need for accountability and transparency exists whether the programmes are in responsive or non-responsive mode. Research Councils and other funding agencies may vary in their emphasis on responsive or non-responsive, therefore it can never be possible to prescribe which approach a researcher may take.

The European Union, for example, is highly directive about its programmes, being specific about its themes and outcomes. At one recent forum to discuss EU research funding, delegates were shocked to be greeted by the opening statement: 'We are not interested in funding your research'. In other words, the EU does not seek partnerships with people who only want to fund their own pet interest or academic speciality. Transparency for the EU will therefore be not just about following guidelines on public spending, but on strictly following its own specifications. One researcher summed up the EU's approach rather negatively: 'They want timesheets'. Another researcher, however, said he admired and preferred the approach precisely because it was so detailed and accountable.

The ESRC, for example, in describing how to apply for EU funding warns that it is different from applying for UK funding, taking more time to develop a proposal and following complex, strictly controlled processes.

Other public bodies, such as the AHRB, work very differently. Apart from one recent collaboration with the ESRC on a themed programme, they will accept research proposals generated from the researcher's own interests, providing they fit its broad strategic objectives. This does not mean, however, that it is opaque. Its evaluation processes are stringent, if not based on timesheets.

The Turn to Collaboration

One of the most significant recent shifts in Research Council funding is its emphasis on collaboration. This implies collaboration amongst disciplines, institutions, governments, countries, and even the Councils themselves.

An important initiative to further the aim of collaboration was the creation in May 2002 of Research Councils UK (RCUK).[4] At the launch, Dr John Taylor, Director General of the Research Councils and Chairman of Research Councils UK, explained that the new body would have three main roles:

---

4   www.research-councils.ac.uk

- defining the strategy for the science budget;
- providing a single voice and single portal to and from the Research Councils' community;
- enabling convergence between the Councils to produce more efficient and effective interfaces, processes and infrastructures.

In practice, researchers may find the site useful for latest research news and for links to the Research Councils. Bodies like RCUK reflect the growing strategic importance of collaboration.

For example, although the ESRC has thematic priorities which covers 65 per cent of its funding, such as Economic Performance and Development, Environment and Human Behaviour, Lifecourse, Lifestyles and Health to name just three of the seven currently available, it also has money for 'responsive mode' through its Research Grants Board, and money for research studentships, all of which will be based on its perceptions of quality and specific relation to its themes. In the themes themselves, it is looking for social science contributions which take historical, comparative and international perspectives and pay attention to theoretical and methodological issues.

Sometimes, the Research Councils collaborate in launching programmes, thus embedding further the notion of interdisciplinary and inter-institutional cooperation. For example, a five-year collaborative research programme in Eating, Food and Health was launched as part of a government LINK initiative. The programme is jointly sponsored by the Economic and Social Research Council, the Biotechnology and Biological Sciences Research Council, the Ministry of Agriculture Fisheries and Food and the Department of Health.

The programme guidelines expressly state that the objective is to encourage a multidisciplinary approach in order to discover more about what influences a healthy diet, including the physiological, sociological and economic perspectives. Its six inter-related themes are designed to provoke involvement amongst biologists, psychologists and social scientists.

Within the context of collaboration, many researchers want to know if they can apply to more than one funder simultaneously. The only answer obvious to anyone who has read thus far is to pose the question: why would you want to? A relationship-based approach is not consistent with trying to cover several options simultaneously, which speaks of both a lack of commitment and lack of discernment. If you have properly targeted your funder, how could there possibly be more than one perfect potential partner?

As the AHRB suggests in its guidance notes:

> It is the view of the Board that applicants
> should be responsible for determining their
> own research priorities, and you should not
> normally submit more than one application in
> any one round.

Charities

Charities in the UK are helping to keep research alive and vibrant, contributing 25 per cent of all research money or nearly £500 million each year. A major difference between a charity and a research council is that the charity does not pay towards the indirect or infrastructure costs of the research project, whereas research councils pay overheads at 46 per cent on staffing costs.

For example, an article in *The Guardian* on 1 March 2002 reported on a Higher Education Funding Council for England (HEFCE) study which suggested that charities 'should contribute more to the full, direct costs of the projects they fund, including the costs of project and staff management'.

Another main difference is that most charities are internally directed by a specific historical ethos which determines their priorities. It may be instructive to look more deeply into the ethos of the Joseph Rowntree Foundation as the largest single funder of social sciences research outside the Research Councils. As its guidance notes describe:

> The Joseph Rowntree Foundation is the
> largest social policy research and
> development charity in the UK. It spends
> about £10 million a year, mostly on a
> research and development programme that
> seeks to better understand the causes of social
> difficulties and explore ways of better
> overcoming them.

Janet Lewis, former Research Director of the Joseph Rowntree Foundation, summed up how the history of the Foundation affects its priorities:

> The way that we operate is that we have
> identified and have had for a long time, a
> number of areas where we have a particular

> interest and it goes back to our history.
> Within those particular areas of interest we
> now mainly fund programmes of work which
> will have a specific topic within a broader
> framework.

This is as a direct result of its historical routes from the Joseph Rowntree Village Trust, set up by Joseph Rowntree, a Quaker, in 1904. He was concerned about housing, conditions and poverty and was determined to fund research into the underlying causes and remedies. Such issues have underpinned the Foundation's themes ever since.

A researcher who understands those roots and ethos will be better placed to work in partnership with the Foundation. They will also pay attention to how that ethos is implemented in practice. The Foundation's 2002 guidance notes are stated in Table 9.1 below.

Table 9.1 Joseph Rowntree Foundation Priorities

General JRF Priorities

A number of interests run through the Foundation's work regardless of the particular subject area and should be taken into account when formulating a proposal for funding.

- **The importance of the perspectives of those being researched.**
- **Race and the issues confronting minority ethnic communities.**
- **A UK perspective.**
- **The rural dimension.**
- **Equal opportunities.**

The Joseph Rowntree Foundation has its origins in the traditions of the Society of Friends (Quakers) and the philosophy of its founder. The Foundation subscribes to a belief in the inherent value of each human being without distinction as to race, gender, age, disability, sexuality or on other grounds. All proposers should, therefore, consider how equal opportunities may relate to the subject being addressed and to the recruitment for and management of the project.

Source: www.jrf.org.uk/funding/applyforfunding/good.asp

The extract illustrates the importance of knowing a funder's history, values and ethos. The Nuffield Foundation was founded by Lord Nuffield, originally William Morris, in 1943 to support work which advanced causes of education or social welfare. The Wellcome Trust was created from the will of Sir Henry Wellcome in 1936. It was established to promote research which improves human and animal health, but elaborates in its guidance notes how those values have evolved through recognising the impact of medicine on society. It is now also focusing on the 'medical, ethical and social implications of research and promotes dialogue between scientists, the public and policy makers.'

The Leverhulme Trust was founded in 1925 through the will of Lord Leverhulme, originally William Hesketh Lever, as an act of philanthropy. Its focus is broader than, for example, the Joseph Rowntree Foundation. People applying to the Leverhulme Trust need to study the specific remits of its various schemes.

Conclusion

The points and sketches above illustrate the importance of familiarising yourself with your funder. The need for a relationship approach exists despite the funder's size or culture. The continuing mantra of 'talk to us' exists in them all. Few researchers understand how vital, and helpful, it often is simply to email or call.

Funding bodies are not remote. The British Academy, for example, has a culture of continuing relationships with researchers, said Dr Ken Emond, of the Research Posts and Academy Research Projects division. The emphasis on direct relationships continues throughout the application and post-award process. People often drop in just to say hello, Dr Emond said, indicating the ongoing interest the Academy and its researchers have in each other.

Researchers report that such relationships and continuity exist with a funding agency even when individuals move. This demonstrates the importance of understanding the body itself, and how its values of history, public accountability or transparency affect its strategic and daily actions.

10 WORKING WITH THE CORPORATE SECTOR

Some academic researchers feel it is their strength with theoretical concepts which attracts the corporate sector, while others think it is their ability to translate general concepts to specific applications. Both are, of course, right. The 'corporate sector' is not an amorphous whole with one specific culture. Different organisations will have different cultures and therefore expectations and ways of behaving will differ.

For many companies, social science is not a recognisable discipline. They think of 'marketing' when they think about people. For others, social science is something loosely about values whereas 'real' science is about facts. Social scientists know that science implicitly includes values and that not everything about society translates to marketing, but the challenge is to talk in the vocabulary the customer understands. Sometimes, this may mean a long process of mutual education, where the academic is learning about the business and the business is learning about academe.

The researchers and their clients who tell their stories below have worked with a variety of organisations across the breadth of industry and services. They have certain experiences and observations in common which relate to risk, time and culture.

Risk is Good

The corporate world is characterised by uncertainty. Markets fluctuate, customers are fickle, suppliers are not always reliable, employees have changing needs. How the corporate world responds to this uncertainty is also subject to change, but the emphasis during the last ten years or so has tended towards 'knowledge management'.

In her book, *Flexible Bodies*, Emily Martin (Martin, 1994) gives a fascinating account of attending a management course involving outdoor activities. The proponents of the method, experiential learning, discussed opening individuals and groups to higher levels of being, of self-actualisation and of experiencing the 'flow'. The resource material stressed the skills of transcending difficult circumstances, of personal transformation and making leaps through unfamiliar territory. The emphasis was on helping workers take personal risks and learning to become independent thinkers, more flexible and agile.

Economies in the G8 countries have now shifted from manufacturing to service businesses, with even manufacturing more dominated by information technology than old-style factories. Just-in-time management requires fast decisions affecting global networks. The shift now is from secondary to tertiary, to the service industry – education, health care, financial services, transportation, entertainment, advertising. These jobs are highly mobile, involve flexible skills and are performed by an elite stratum of people called knowledge workers.

The corporate sector, if it can be generalised at all, is generalised by this thirst for knowledge. To dismiss it as a sector requiring only short-term, fast-buck solutions would be to seriously underestimate its combined intelligence and trajectory. The large organisations which pour millions into graduate recruitment programmes are not doing so lightly. As one senior executive dryly commented: 'There are probably more PhDs in our organisation than most universities.'

Being an academic simply working on theory is not, for many researchers, enough. The theory part is what academics are trained to do: it is a necessary but insufficient condition of academic excellence in many disciplines. Said one experienced researcher, Professor Mohamed Zairi, Director of the European Centre for Total Quality Management at Bradford University:

> We do the conceptual stuff because it's a licence to practice. Every academic knows how to do research, how to read the literature, how to design questionnaires and how to do survey questionnaires.

The valuable point, in his view, is to go further, to experience a cycle of theory-to-practice-to-evaluation-and-back again, all within a climate of uncertainty. He expands on this:

> The academic does not start with the solution; this is wrong. You start with the unknown, the problem. You ask the customer: what is the problem, what do you want to do, what do you want to get out of it, how are we going to help you?

This experience, in his view, is one that requires practice. The more you do that, the better you become: 'It's like coaching somebody to perfect their shooting ability or the way they kick a ball,' he says. Where else will an academic receive that coaching but the 'real world'? Academics may read books or papers for stimulation, Mohamed argues, but stimulation is not directed: 'It just opens your mind by telling you – look, there is another angle, there is another idea, but that's not testing.'

Testing theoretical concepts is, in his view, critical, whether it is a natural science or social sciences or engineering: 'We must test our knowledge.' When he looks at a client, he sees an opportunity for testing that in a real environment, because the clients are the ones who live the reality:

> They live the problem every day. They are
> the ones who have to deliver to their real
> customers. And that must be preserved. So
> that's what partnership is. It's all of these
> things put together.

This view is emphasised by Nirex Communications and Decision Analyst, Elizabeth Atherton:

> If you're using academics, they're interested
> not just in the products or knowledge but how
> they got there. You get that added analysis.
> We're always trying to learn the lessons. It
> helps us know we are doing the theoretical
> best we can do.

In her job, the added value of an academic is important, particularly if they have a background in the social sciences. As she explains: 'All problems are not technical. Most have a social dimension.' Although Nirex, whose business is managing radioactive waste, undoubtedly has some of the finest scientists working on the most excruciatingly complex problems, this expertise alone is sometimes not enough.

Asked what in her view were the attributes of an academic who successfully works within her industry, she replied with four clear characteristics:

- someone who can understand the situation you're facing;
- someone who can tap into problems you haven't told them about but that exist;
- someone who is not afraid of learning something new;
- someone who shares your values – in this case, about public consultation.

That may sound like a tall order, but it is hardly unfamiliar to an experienced academic. If those points are what a corporate partner is looking for and why, what is the attraction for the academic? It is probably not just money, particularly considering one senior executive's off-hand remark that an advantage of using academic researchers is that 'they're cheaper than consultants'. (Problems of under-valuing, and potentially under-charging, were discussed in an earlier chapter.) The benefits academic researchers gain from work in the corporate sector appear to be richer than even the monetary reward.

Intellectualism combined with entrepreneurial verve attracts academic researchers like Dr Phil Macnaghten from the Centre for the Study of Environmental Change at Lancaster University. Referring to the academic world in general, he says: 'There's a tremendous kind of conservatism, probably more than in the corporate sector, where so many things get into the "too difficult" box.'

In the corporate sector, by contrast, it may take just one person to become interested in an idea to open it further for exploration. Sometimes, this seems refreshingly different from the public sector's emphasis on reviewers, outcomes and users. In the corporate sector, the relationship between client and researcher can set new ideas rapidly in motion, as Phil notes: 'It's much more of a co-partnership type exercise where you're both making it up at the same time, a kind of fluid dynamic relationship, which I think tends to be more productive.'

He advises approaching a prospective relationship from a position of strength, ensuring that you retain your own intellectual identity and independence. This is not as difficult as it may sound, he says, once people realize that working with the corporate sector is not just a matter of helping them sell products. Rather, he argues that the role for academics is to be part of a current expanding process which explores the role of business in society and wider dynamics of governance, power, and the role of the nation state.

Dr Zahir Irani, of Brunel University, says it is the opportunity to do applied research which attracts him to the corporate sector. He rarely does pure, theoretical research anymore, mainly for two main reasons. Firstly, he finds it more difficult to publish: 'I can't push theoretical ideas – everyone's got a good idea. I think you're increasingly seeing departments of this size handling more and more and more applied work.' Secondly, because it is theoretical he finds it has little industrial significance, which means it is unlikely to receive corporate funding:

You're never going to get a collaborator that
wants to sit and discuss hypothetical
situations. I would say in my opinion to be a
five or a five star, you could only be doing
applied work, because otherwise you will just
not get industrial collaborators. You will not
get them involved, and increasingly the RAE
is looking for the amount of such
collaboration – not only money spent, but the
level of industrial collaboration, and also the
level of industry funding you get, which is a
barometer to how successful you are in doing
research.

Risking Reputation

Academic researchers who engage in those relationships know that they come
with risks. Some people think to work with industry may risk academic
credibility. Phil Macnaghten says he considered this at first, but with
experience does not perceive it as necessarily a problem. He identifies two
risks: the risk of association, and the risk of becoming too immersed in the
problem itself. The way he overcame those risks was to develop the right kind
of relationships, both with the corporate world and with others related to the
same issue. In the case of Unilever and his funded project on genetically
modified foods, the research team remained engaged with both the corporate
client and with the contact group – a group of environmental and consumer
Non-Government Organisations (NGOs) convened for Unilever by the
environmental charity, the Green Alliance.

As Phil points out, everyone involved was taking a risk, not just the university:
'We responded to it because we trusted the process and we trusted the
individuals who were involved in the process, and the risk that they were
taking,' he explains, underlining again the nature of research being a
partnership.

Mohamed Zairi agrees that some people may raise the issue of academic
credibility, but it is one he dismisses, because 'it doesn't make sense'. Quite
apart from one's adherence to ethics and standards, compromise in favour of
sponsorship would thwart everyone's objectives: 'The truth of the matter is,
industry or practitioners are not there to compromise your credibility or your
thinking.' If either the client or the academic did so, both would lose their

credibility in their chosen fields and damage their careers or reputations. As in most fields, reputation is all. Says Mohamed:

> To me, that's something I cherish. What I've accomplished, my name out there in the field, is something I will never compromise.

Time

Some academics feel compromised by time pressures. One of the unavoidable aspects of corporate life is a deadline focus. This may lead some academics to feel pushed into short-term solutions, which in turn may aggravate a sense of compromise.

One experienced researcher described the industry cycle travelling at 200 miles an hour whereas academics travel at 10 miles an hour. This may be because many academics are driven by a need for accuracy, verifiable data and a sense of completeness or even perfection before submitting a report, in the same way that many resist submitting papers for publication before they are perfect. Other researchers point out that academics today are also working in a more time-sensitive environment. They, too, operate under constraints and time pressures.

The real difference may not be the corporate tendency to short-termism, but precisely the opposite. The long-term view for a corporate entity is often more long-term than many academics will ever experience. Reflecting on the world of corporate clients in the mining and oil industry, one researcher pointed out that they are thinking about what the world will be like in 20 or 50 years' time.

Elizabeth Atherton at Nirex agrees that the decision-making process can span decades. Her organisation would be looking for research to influence not only what happens now but far into the future. This forces a new academic researcher into a sharp learning curve and explains why the successful ones tend to form deep and long-term relationships with their clients.

Rather than think of a corporation as not having a long-term view, it may be more realistic to see how their long term is collapsed into a series of short-term stages. Researchers who conclude that corporations 'think' in short bursts of days or months, may in fact be only seeing one small part of a longer project.

Where does that leave the academic feeling under pressure to produce a short-term solution? Most researchers will say that depends on the problem and the relationship. In a long-term relationship there may, indeed, be short projects which require more immediate attention than others, and an academic research partner may often contribute to them. In practice, however, these are usually accompanied by long-term projects operating simultaneously. Some researchers see these as a dual track system within the same organisation – a fast track and a slow track. An academic researcher in a long-term relationship may need to deliver both.

Dissemination Issues

What kind of ownership should a corporate body have over your work? This is a question of 'intellectual property' which will vary according to the client. Commercially sensitive information may be embargoed for a long time, whereas general overviews or theoretical analysis may not be.

Permission to publish is not always a problem, although it should always form part of the negotiation. Phil Macnaghten at Lancaster says that it was a condition of the research team's work with Unilever that the company would not oppose publication.

> One of the conditions of doing the work was
> that we had full editorial control. It's our work
> and the only reason that this process could
> work with integrity is if we were independent
> and seen to be independent.

Unilever not only accepted that, they paid for a print run of 3 000. Although reports may not have the same perceived status as peer review papers, Phil thinks this is a nonsense. Their report, *Uncertain World*, had a print run double that of most academic books, but its message also penetrated policy processes and made a contribution towards the framing of the national policy debate on GM foods: it had an effect. This, in his mind, compensates for the lack of recognition in some academic circles:

> The translation of our work into standard
> journals has suffered and again it's because
> our focus has been on change and working on
> real world issues – it's not so much on writing
> peer review journal articles.

Although the Research Assessment Exercise specifically mentions that it will accept company reports and unpublished confidential reports, many peer reviewers in practice do not regard them highly. Although some people suggest that this is changing, there still remains a problem with the time lag between submission and eventual publication in traditional journals, which may be as much as two years. There is arguably a need for a system of quality control which could see papers reviewed and published within a few months, and thus remain timely.

Different Culture

In the corporate market, academics may find they are competing with consultants who have a different approach to research. This approach may seem more appropriate to certain corporate cultures which warmly accept a two-day research job culminating in a 'literature review' and analysis.

If the academic is not careful to articulate the value of more in-depth research, consultants can seem like an attractive option. This is not because they are cheaper – they are usually more expensive – but because they often fit into corporate culture more easily than an academic researcher.

Firstly, a consultant tends to look more like the client. One researcher described the stereotype of academics from the perspective of the corporate sector as 'people who turn up in corduroy trousers'. Consultants don't wear corduroy trousers, they wear suits. This translates in the corporate sector as professionalism. So what is an academic researcher to do? Jane Hunt's response, as described earlier, was to buy a suit.

Another cultural difference is the vocabulary. Academics and corporate clients tend to talk differently, using different words and syntax. That is partly explained by affinity theory: people will talk like those around them. It's a reflection of the world in which they move. Another explanation, however, resounds with the core purpose of what many academics are trying to achieve. There is sometimes an absence of vocabulary within the corporate sector for phenomena which the academic understands and is trying to describe.

As one researcher said about a corporate client: 'What we were offering to them was a different type of vocabulary to help them understand the social and political dynamics and their implications for a major corporate actor.'

Knowing that a different vocabulary is necessary is one thing; imposing it on the client at the outset is quite another, and usually ineffective, option. Jane

Hunt, for example, noticed that Nirex did not have a website, which in her view contradicted their apparent aim towards more openness and public accountability. She might describe the website as something which opened the door into a new social-cultural perspective, but how did she describe it to the client? 'I called it a website,' she answered.

Other cultural differences are reflected in how companies pay their contractors. Many academic researchers find it difficult to account for their work in terms of hours rather than final reports. This is where the university's research office will be able to help.

Conclusion

The 'corporate sector' is not a homogeneous mass, full of people who look and act the same. Some corporations plan and invest only as far as next month; some, fifty years ahead. Some firms have barely an A-level between them; others employ more PhDs than most universities. It is very important not to think about dealing with the corporate world by using a single, one-size-fits-all approach.

One thing successful companies do tend to have in common is a thirst for knowledge about their markets, customers, competitors, business processes, environments and staff. Most of us now work in the 'knowledge economy', employing 'knowledge workers'. Most managers in businesses can use and understand concepts like 'knowledge management', 'knowledge assets' and 'intellectual capital'.

This of course is good news to those interested in working on funded research with the corporate sector. For who better to participate in knowledge creation and application than a successful partnership of scholarly researcher and company management team. Elizabeth Atherton of Nirex talked about the 'added analysis' of a scholarly researcher's approach in looking at the process and methodology of coming to a conclusion. This kind of 'added analysis', which a skilled academic research team can bring, makes for better and more robust decisions.

The benefits can be felt the other way too. Many researchers enjoy the decision-focus and entrepreneurial energy which can come from working with a good corporate client. Also, there is usually an obvious and tangible result to corporate-funded research. It usually gets applied in some way.

One point to take note of is that a university will generally feel like a different environment from a company. It is worth spending some time trying to absorb the corporate culture and expected norms of your 'client' firm, from language, to dress code, to meeting behaviour. The creativity which comes when academic researchers meet corporate sponsors is one of the reasons why companies invest in academic research. You are not expected to become an employee overnight. But in terms of competing for, then nurturing a relationship, it is sensible, as one might say in the business world, to 'be where your customers are'.

PART *III*

BUILDING THE RESEARCH PARTNERSHIP

11 ASSESSING PARTNER NEEDS

Successful researchers become adept at finding out as much as possible about a potential funding partner before they decide to submit a proposal. It is tempting, when faced with the time pressures that any busy person has, to neglect doing detailed homework on a funding partner before completing an application. But as we have discussed, and will go on to discuss further, a research application is not an abstract entity, to be judged on 'its own merits'. It will be judged against how well it appears to deliver against a funder's objectives. Therefore, no assessment, or a superficial assessment of the funder's needs, is likely to lead to problems and disappointments further down the line.

The first stage of needs assessment is to become clear about the many different groups involved in what may appear to be a single funding organisation. Every organisation, of any kind, is involved in a hierarchy of relationships of which potential partners would be advised to become aware.

An important principle of needs analysis is the creation of a picture of the organisation's relationships. Start at the lowest unit of analysis and work up and outwards. One way of describing this activity is 'stakeholder analysis'.

Understanding Multiple Needs

If, for example, you are contemplating submitting a proposal for a particular project programme within a public body, such as the ESRC or AHRB, your first question should be: how does this affect the needs of everyone involved? Research councils have multiple stakeholders to satisfy. One set of stakeholders is the academic researchers and students they fund. Another set is the users of their research – in a sense, the customers and consumers of the research outputs – such as private or public bodies. Another group of stakeholders are policymakers – the funding bodies' own funding decision-makers, ultimately going to top levels in government. Yet another set is the media and wider public, who can have an influence, positively or negatively, on how politicians come to see research funding as a worthwhile investment as judged by their constituents. For some funders, particularly charities, the beneficiaries of the research are important stakeholders.

All of these relationships and interrelationships can be explored through reading the funder's strategic plan, which formulates and expresses corporate aims and objectives for activities that meet the aspirations, requirements and needs of those multiple stakeholders.

The researcher may look at the work purely from an individual or a team's point of view, whereas the funder must look at the researcher as a member in a community. This is something many people ignore, concentrating instead on how their project may enhance their own work or reputation but not how it may contribute to the programme as a whole. Commitment to the entire programme and its objectives and all those involved is a critical consideration. To be of value to the funder and its communities, the research must reflect the aims of the specific scheme within which an award is being sought, as well as the wider strategic aims of the funder. Knowing this and articulating it may make the final difference between equal, alpha-graded applications. This would apply equally to single research grants as to projects within large programmes.

Private sector organisations also have multiple stakeholders, including shareholders, staff, customers, the media, industry groups, legal and regulatory bodies, potential employees, pension fund investors and competitors.

Elizabeth Atherton, Communications and Decision Analyst at Nirex, says that involving academics from disparate fields is a specific way to ensure the needs of different groups are met.

'We wanted to tap into an existing organisation with links to stakeholder groups,' she explained. No one organisation can be sure it understands the more complex needs of all those affected by its work, so contracting with academics who have those networks is of specific value. The challenge for the academic researcher who is seeking funding, is being able to recognise and convince the funder of their ability to add that value.

Knowing the Reviewers

Who will be involved in decisions about a research proposal? There is no standard answer to that question, as it varies from funder to funder, but it can certainly be discovered. One way of doing so is often via a website. Another is by simply asking the question. The differences between reviewers can be significant but your question is always the same: what do they need, and how can I satisfy them?

When proposals come into an office, staff members look at them and thus become active in the process of reviewing. They will weed out – sometimes with external advice, sometimes on their own – the weaker proposals. This is not too difficult a process, as so many proposals are haphazardly conceived, badly written, poorly expressed and bear no relationship to the needs of the funder.

The most remote group in the assessment process seems to be that which is known as 'peer reviewers'. These are experts in the field chosen to assess applications in the different subject areas. Many researchers talk about peer reviewers in hushed, reverent tones, as if they are numinous creatures beyond human understanding. This assumption is quite inappropriate once you realise that peer reviewers are ordinary people, many of whom you probably know and meet at conferences every year. It is usually a simple process to find out who the peer reviewers are. Subject areas or specific schemes will often have panels and the membership of the panels is, in the case of a public body, publicly accessible.

It is more constructive to think of peer reviewers as people who have needs to be met rather than as impartial gatekeepers to the academic body of knowledge. What might they be looking for? What do they sense in the body of knowledge is missing? Why would they want you to become a member of their academic community?

Knowing Their Needs Before They Do

In the Unilever example explored in earlier chapters, it was the researchers' view initially, not the company's, that the genetically-modified foods issue should be explored. The researchers anticipated social dynamics which had not yet registered in the industry, but they needed empirical evidence and a genuine example to explore. Unilever gave them that opportunity and in so doing radically influenced its own and the industry's policies.

Dr Phil Macnaghten from the Centre for the Study of Environmental Change at Lancaster University (CSEC), describes needs assessment as something that changes as the relationship continues. This reflects much of the theme of this book: one-off transactions are not as helpful for forming an enduring understanding of the partner as are long-term relationships. This was particularly marked in his relationship with Unilever which he describes as mutually respectful and in an important sense independent.

> It only works well when there isn't a kind of
> relationship of dependency, so I think when

one or other side tends to feeling a
dependency that's when the quality of the
research can be reduced or the integrity can
go or you can find yourself asking questions
which you don't feel particularly happy with.
A lot of the ways in which the research pans
out is actually a process of translation. You
translate what they think they want to know
into what you think they should think they
should want to know. It's actually a
negotiation and I think it's important that that
negotiation happens not from a sense of
being terribly dependent. That's why we
pride ourselves on what we do, adding a kind
of bona fide, open, intellectual, academic
quality to it.

Professor Mohamed Zairi, Director of the European Centre for Total Quality
Management at Bradford, offers another concrete example. One of his
sponsors was the Research Development Centre of a major corporation.
They wanted the research team to do a benchmarking study in the area of
internal project management and innovation. The timescale for doing this
complex project was four months, which Mohamed thought was ambitious,
but agreed to take it on condition that the client would increase the budget to
allow for extra resources.

To start the project, the research team ran an initial workshop with the client
management and asked a simple question: had they evaluated their processes
internally? Had they documented them, and created a standard of
performance? Had they, for example, tracked a number of projects that had
run on schedule and behind schedule, and had they evaluated the reasons
behind those delays? Had they, for example, tracked projects that have been
culled and the reasons why they have been terminated? Mohamed recalls
'they looked at me in shock and horror because they hadn't done this baseline
work'.

He explained to them that one of the fundamental principles of
benchmarking is that you must do the internal diagnosis and document your
standard of performance to answer the question, where are we now? The
client agreed that such work needed to be done, which delayed the project by
nine months, but gave the research team the information they needed to do a
proper job in the four months they had agreed.

The project was completed successfully and is now a published case study. The most important part for Mohamed is that the client's original timescale could be shifted, in favour of the methodological rigour needed to get a really useful result from the programme. The end product was that their real need was satisfied in ways they had not anticipated originally.

> This is an example where your integrity as a thinker, as an academic, is not compromised. People will respect your views because you have educated them into a process which is rigorous, which is scientific and you have basically demonstrated to them that they cannot go any further without doing this in this way.

Jane Hunt, contract researcher at Lancaster University, developed her relationship with Nirex by spotting a need before the organisation had seen it. She suggests that a good way to do so is to go where the potential funder is and assess their needs from there, perhaps at a conference. In her area, it is not difficult to find people who may need to focus on the issues she thinks are important. Like most businesses and industries, members of the nuclear industry have conferences. Academic researchers who want to change the way organisations behave will need to find them where they congregate, and share their ideas and problems. From spotting the need there becomes an action to follow, perhaps a discussion that may begin as simply as 'Can I talk to you?'

Peter Townsend, Research Manager at Loughborough University, says that a good way to find out what people really want is to 'read between the lines'. The best way to learn what lies between the lines is to meet people. Information days, seminars, or conferences, offer good opportunities to talk with prospective funders and discover the nuances in the official regulations. Talking to a programme director, for example, may reveal more about what is being sought than the public guidelines can possibly cover.

Other details may emerge which can affect the likelihood of receiving funding at any particular time. The organisation may be coming to the end of its financial year, for example, and certain programmes may be oversubscribed, while other programmes have not spent their budget. No one wants a budget to be under-spent, because this will normally mean that next year's budget will be reduced. As we mentioned in Chapter 1, one of the most important performance measures for a funding body is whether and how well they have spent their research budget. No one judges good performance as having not spent the expected amount of money. It is their job to do so.

While academic researchers cannot be expected to attend external events on a regular basis, research administrators, business development officers and research managers in the university will normally make it their business to be there.

This raises an interesting point which we have raised in other chapters: people employed as research officers or research administrators have normally gained a wealth of knowledge about funders which funding applicants can draw on.

Talk to Them

There is no better way to assess someone's needs than to talk to them about it. This seems like an obvious point but many people seem unwilling to do it, for all sorts of reasons. It may be habit or fear. It may be reticence and not wishing to seem 'pushy'. It may be a kind of arrogance which says that the researcher's own ideas and reputation will be sufficient. As we have seen already in this work, that is the kind of attitude that invites application rejection, not acceptance.

'Talk to us!' is the constant refrain from research funders. Everyone from the Leverhulme Trust to the ESRC to the local representative office for the European Union has said the same thing without exception: 'Tell your readers that they can always talk to us.'

How do you know who to talk to? This will vary between organisations, but at the very least there will be someone's name against a programme or department somewhere on a website. Start with them. If they're not the right person, they will tell you who is.

In the private sector, it may be more difficult to find the right person as they will likely not have a website with a list of pre-established programmes. The suggestion of going to a conference, discussed earlier, is a good starting point. The next stage is follow-through. If you have received someone's business card, phone them. If they do not return the call phone them again. Send them an email. Ask them for an appointment.

If you do not know who to talk to, start at the lowest level possible. Don't expect to go directly to the chief executive or head of research. At the beginning of the relationship you will not be aware of their internal politics and you will therefore find it impossible to judge who to talk to. One experienced researcher told me that it is often better to 'go in via a junior who can show you around rather than straight to the top when you might make mistakes. Don't go in cold.' Over time, through building up experience and relationship, you won't have to 'go in cold'. People will come to you.

Sometimes, it is during the period following a proposal submission that you have the opportunity to meet face to face. David Crowther, Research Director at the University of North London Business School, says that sometimes the funder will want to meet the researchers specifically to ask them to resubmit a proposal. This may be because the original proposal was nearly close enough to their needs to be acceptable but needs a slight variation, or it may be because their needs have changed in the meantime.

Finally, to really meet someone's needs, action must happen. Thinking about it and talking about it is not action, it's fantasy. What will really happen?

'I think it's called closing', said one researcher, invoking the parlance of the sales and marketing industry. But it's the right parlance. Somewhere along the way someone has to bring the discussion to a conclusion. As the same researcher noted:

> Academics are used to having long,
> interesting discussions that don't always end.
> They need to learn how to leave with
> something defined. That's often an
> agreement to put some idea together and get
> back. Research experience helps: it's a matter
> of writing to them, following up, making
> phone calls – pinning them down!

Conclusion

Any organisation which hands out funding for research has to satisfy a number of people and other entities to whom they are accountable in some way, or who have some kind of interest in what they are doing. Thinking about the needs and perceptions of these stakeholders – including the academic research community, investors, staff, customers, the media, government policymakers, civil servants, legal and regulatory bodies, and potential employees – can be helpful in framing a successful proposal.

Information on a funding partner's needs, ambitions and stakeholders can often be found with a little diligent homework. Look at any public domain information available, in a library or on a website.

It is useful to look for and attend the right kind of conferences, seminars or open days, when a lot of useful information and contacts can be gleaned.

Many funders say, quite simply, talk to us! Contact us, by email, telephone or in person. The more you find out about what we want, they say, the more closely your application is likely to match our needs. Less wasted time for all of us!

12 MANAGING YOUR PERSONAL PROFILE

Many people working in academic research positions take their expertise for granted. After all, if they were not well-qualified, why else would they be on the staff of a respectable university, or published in a reputable journal? Their background and suitability for the project must, they may think, be self-evident.

Winning and losing in research funding applications is not just a matter of luck, of being in the right place at the right time. As we have explored in this book, the evidence is that luck has something, but only a little, to do with it. As the great professional golfer Lee Trevino once said, after an interviewer's comment that he was 'lucky' in a competition he had just won, 'Yes, it's funny. The more I practise, the luckier I get!' Of course, everyone who reaches the very highest levels of achievement, in whatever field, will have had a rich slice of luck along the way. And many who may be equally skilled or brilliant or deserving may have failed to get a lucky break at the right time. There is nothing you can do about that. It is, as scientists might say, a variable which cannot be controlled for. But, by and large, you make your own luck – meaning that there are many variables which can be controlled and managed.

It is perhaps more accurate to think of a funding application as a game, rather than a gamble. As anyone who has ever played a game understands, just knowing the rules is not enough. Winning happens more consistently after we practise, discover our style and achieve finesse. We do not break the rules or win by surreptitious means, but we understand and play them to our advantage. As one successful researcher, Dr Zairi Irani at Brunel University aptly put it:

> I think the process is a game and I think the reality of it is that you either play only by the rules and lose more than you win, or you play the game by understanding the rules better. You're still going to lose sometimes, but you get a better chance of winning. You've got to work out the game, work out the rules

> because we're people, we're humans, we have
> our allegiances, we have our abilities to work
> within guidelines and yet we also have
> abilities to be sympathetic to external factors
> and you've got to recognise that.

In this chapter, we will assume that part of the 'rules' is being able to adequately demonstrate fully who you are. We will assume that nothing is self-evident. Rather, we will explore how to present your profile, including how you present yourself, your team and your institution. The main objective here is not to depend on the prospective funder somehow luckily working out how right you are for the project, but that you will be managing that presentation so they will find it difficult to draw any other conclusion.

Getting Beyond Luck

It may be that you formulate a research proposal, or see an invitation to tender, and think 'Yes! That is such a good fit for me! I believe that right now, I really am the best-placed person in the world to do this specific piece of research.' You may be right, but several problems may nevertheless arise:

- Three hundred other people also believe they are the best in the world are applying for the same grant.
- Two hundred of those really *are*, equally, the best suited in the world.
- One hundred and fifty of these have submitted accurate application forms and a proposal which matches the funder's specifications.
- One hundred of you have aligned your work to the aims and objectives of the funding agency, thereby emerging as a perfect candidate.
- Fifty of you have also created a faultless budget.
- There is only enough money for ten of you.

Apart from the critical success factors we have reviewed so far, what else can push you into the top ten? Let us not worry now about luck. You can't manage luck. Let us concentrate on the variables which can be managed.

Busy staff and busy panellists will not always be attuned to the nuances and implications of your application. Yes, if they read your cv carefully and calculate the dates it will become obvious that you are one of the youngest professors in your field. If they add up your publications and divide that number by the number of years in which you have been research-active it will be apparent that you have published significantly more than might have been expected. If they look into the background of your referees they will see you have selected people who actively engage with your research areas but who have also constructively criticised them, and therefore they will see you as a highly respected and credible academic. And so on.

The problem is that in practice the busy staff and busy panellists will often not conduct that level of exploration. And, indeed, why should they? There may be a group of people whose suitability is obvious at first glance. Those people will be noticed not only because their suitability has been articulated, but because the busy staff member or panellist will appreciate the effort the applicant took to do so. With whom would you rather have a relationship? Someone who makes life difficult for you, or easier?

One time when I was running a research and consulting business I placed a small advertisement in the national press for two research assistants. Over the next two weeks, we received 400 applications. As the mail arrived in ever-increasing piles – 30 letters and cvs one day, 50 the next – we resorted to a very expedient selection process. Anything which didn't make an impression within about ten seconds didn't make the cut. Anything which did went onto a much-reduced pile which got a second, longer, read-through, until we got down to a short list of six whom we interviewed.

The point of the story is that I also had a business to run. There may well have been a collection of gems buried in the applications but I had no time to read them, think about them and uncover them. Just like our example above, imagine the sheer practicalities of reducing 300 good-looking, long and complex applications down to ten. Now imagine it when you are a research director with other project teams to manage, with staff who phone in sick, and when you are trying to sort out the delivery of your new washing machine which is already three days late. Because research funding decision-makers are just people, like you and me, with a whole range of complicated decision priorities. Your funding application may be the most important priority in your life right now, but it is certainly not the most important thing in theirs!

There are several attributes of your background which the funding agency needs to know and feel reassured about. Of these, two were frequently cited by researchers and funding bodies I interviewed: experience and enthusiasm.

Experience Counts

Many new researchers face a seemingly impossible hurdle: research funding agencies will want to see a track record of research experience from prospective researchers, many of whom will not have the experience. How, therefore, will a new, inexperienced researcher gain necessary research experience? It is not only new researchers who face this difficulty. Experienced researchers may not properly present their experience or their university's stature and therefore may be overlooked.

The best way to gain research experience is to do it, any of it. This may mean starting small and building your portfolio, but every small part will eventually combine into a bigger picture. New researchers are often advised to start small, mainly because chances are better that you will be accepted when the stakes are not so high. This means bidding for comparatively small amounts of money – an award to attend a conference, for example, or a small grant of less than £1 000 either through an external agency or an internal university programme.

Do not overlook or under-value internal research programmes. A university award is an important measure of your research potential. Being recognised and rewarded by your peers is an accolade. Some universities make it a highly competitive undertaking.

At the University of Sunderland, for example, a tight process governs internal funding. Rather than divide research money across schools, to be distributed amongst departments, each department and individuals wanting research money must advance a justifiable case. Simon Kerridge, Deputy Director of the university's Graduate Research School, says this is not a typical university model, but he thinks it encourages a better outcome than one which merely sustains the status quo.

Simon explained that because the university was previously a polytechnic, it had little research experience when it became a university. Creating a central research support unit and a strategic approach to funding was a deliberate move to enhance research expertise and experience. The contribution of the team has been significant: research income has increased ten-fold during the past five years.

Putting together a plan for your research to be funded internally is very similar to creating a proposal for external funding. In this case, the experience of creating winning proposals will be rewarding as it improves your chances of creating further winning proposals. Receiving the money for your internal work can represent research success and experience to the outside world.

Experience is therefore something which can be gained from numerous sources, apart from external funding bodies. One way is to join initiatives in the university which encourage research. These may be linked to the

Teaching and Learning Research programmes, or to technology transfer schemes. For example, many researchers learn about research and its applications through participating in the Teaching Company scheme. This allows small- to medium-sized businesses to employ a researcher through government subsidy.

Another way to gain experience is to participate in pre-research activities. Does your department have a group which helps prepare their departmental plan? Are you a member of that group? If not, why not? Find out what it takes to be considered to be a member and do what is necessary. What other committees or consultative groups exist in your university? While participation in these groups may seem like a boring, administrative chore, joining them will demonstrate several aspects of your profile which will be attractive to others. It will show you have experience in, amongst other things:

- Planning
- Strategic thinking
- Collaboration
- Teamwork
- Administration
- Project management
- Leadership
- Specific subject groups.

These are, of course, the skills funders seek from prospective research partners.

Contributing to your field of knowledge can be exercised in ways outside your immediate university. What, for example, are the relevant academic or professional bodies to which you might belong? Do you belong? Why not? If you do belong, what are that body's specific tasks with which you can become involved?

This participation will not only bring you the rewards of experience, it may position you as someone to whom external bodies will come for advice. Public bodies, in particular, have an obligation to include the ideas, opinions and needs of a variety of stakeholders. Before schemes are finalised, the funding agency will have conducted wide-ranging consultation amongst its several stakeholders – academics and students, users of the research such as private or public bodies, policymakers and the media and wider public.

This is the ultimate status for researcher involvement: be one of those who sets the agenda, makes the rules and creates the guidelines. Why be one of the hundreds of people passively applying for money when you could be one of those influencing which programmes or strategies are adopted by the funder in the first place?

A particular researcher might be just the right person at the right time to meet a specific need in a certain stage of a longer process. The skill, and hard work, is to assess, through analysis and consultation, exactly what that need may be.

The ability to manage one's own profile and career is an essential skill sought by funding agencies even at the earlier stages of an academic's career. In the AHRB notes to Ph.D. students, for example, the characteristics of such management are articulated clearly. They expect a student to be able to:

- appreciate the need for and show commitment to continued professional development
- take ownership for and manage one's career progression, set realistic and achievable career goals, and identify and develop ways to improve employability
- demonstrate an insight into the transferable nature of research skills to other work environments and the range of career opportunities within and outside academia
- present one's skills, personal attributes and experiences through effective cvs, applications and interviews.

Showing Enthusiasm

One feature which distinguishes the ordinary from the exceptional researcher is enthusiasm. Funders like to work with people who are excited about their work. Doesn't everyone? Just doing the job that needs to be done is hardly inspiring. Most of us who work in fields of academic research and study do it because we want to, even because we love to. Being able to demonstrate and communicate that enthusiasm may require a little effort. Too often, we mistakenly conclude that the only professional manner is one which is subdued and careful, but we all know in our own lives how contagious and invigorating enthusiastic people really are.

Nobody, however, can communicate enthusiasm by staying safely behind a computer screen or desk. Showing enthusiasm means being able to reach out to people and let them feel that you are excited about working with them. That means being visible. Being visible can occur in many venues. Some funders will turn to people they know already and just pick up the phone, invite them to come over for a chat, and happily explore prospects for future research. Particularly for private sector organisations, why go through a complex tendering task if you know who to talk to?

Researchers awaiting that enviable position can still ensure that chat happens by picking up the phone themselves. If you have come across something interesting about an organisation that stimulates your researcher's creative urges, why not tell them? This means reading the right papers, journals or magazines that correspond with the interests of your prospective funder. Pick up the phone, talk to them, go see them.

For some organisations, the search is continually on to find new and exciting partners. Those bodies act proactively, looking for people at conferences, on the internet, through published work. They want to see people who are committed to the field and therefore actively participating in it – not only at the typical season of academic conferences but at industry-related or trade conferences. Few academics bother to turn up at such commercial events, therefore the ones who do are noticed and assumed to be interested.

Another way to gain experience and demonstrate enthusiasm is to help organise seminars or conferences. This not only gives you all the experience just mentioned, but it allows you to widen your personal network and meet people with whom you can collaborate. If you actively seek to develop your personal profile and make yourself known and visible in the right places, and to the right people, they will be attracted to you. Winning research funding is therefore positioned as not just a desperate attempt to beg people for money, but a continuous effort and awareness that, as the old saying goes, 'you are known by the friends that you make and the company you keep'. The value of a strong profile and good reputation will help assure that your funding partnerships are mutually beneficial.

Conclusion

Luck may be a part of success in winning funded research, but you will not get anywhere if you are just hoping to be lucky. There are many variables in getting your research proposal noted that can be successfully managed. These are the ones we are interested in.

It is important to demonstrate how well you, as a researcher and a member of a research team, match the priorities and ambitions of a funder. You are, in reality, dealing with busy people who often have a mountain of applications to work through and evaluate, as well as other priorities in their work and their lives. So make noticing you easy for them to do. They won't always take the time to find the nuggets of gold hidden away in an application.

Two criteria are predominant amongst the rest in getting a funding application on to a shortlist and then accepted. These are experience and enthusiasm.

If you don't have good experience, you need to get some! Start small. Help out on research projects which are already ongoing. Do internally funded research. Join planning or management teams. Find some things to list on your cv which will position you as a valuable member of a research team. Experience says not that you might be able to do it, but that you have actually done it.

Everyone likes to work with enthusiasts. If you are out for a meal, you want to have waiting staff who are clearly taking great efforts to make sure your food is on time and presented well, and that your needs are taken care of. If you are part of the decision-making body in a charitable trust trying to make the world a better place by funding research which will make a difference to people, you want to be working with people who seem to share that same burning ambition, who look like they will go an extra mile.

So work on projects you feel passionate about and are really committed to. Be visible. Engage with people. Enthusiasm shines through.

13 WRITING PROPOSALS

This chapter explores several key success factors in writing proposals. The 'proposal' stage comes late in the process. By the time you get to write a proposal, you should be clear about who your funder is, what is required and how you need to position your work.

Each proposal is unique. You may be creating this as a reply to an invitation to tender, or because you think your research matches a specific scheme. Alternatively, you may be submitting this after understanding a particular organisation's issues, in which case this follows a lengthy exploration of someone's needs.

There is, therefore, no single 'right' way to write a proposal – no pro forma or standard structure which can simply be photocopied, filled in and submitted. The purpose of this chapter is to summarise some of the key points which winning proposals appear to have in common. Remember, always, that there are equally good proposals flooding into your prospective funder's office every day. Think of what the ESRC says when it advises candidates in its guidance notes:

> To make your proposal stand out from the
> scores of other applications that will land on
> the assessors' desks, you will have to pay
> particular attention to the way that you write
> and present it.

When considering your proposal, look to see if it addresses three main issues:

- Research question
- Context
- Method

The best proposals respond to those questions concisely and with timescales. Not addressing them is the most common cause, according to the AHRB, of application failure. The following extract from its guidance notes make that clear:

- It must define a series of **research questions** that will be addressed or problems that will be explored in the course of the research. It must also define its objectives in terms of answering those questions, or reporting on the results of the investigation.
- It must specify a **research context** for the questions to be addressed or problems to be explored. You must specify why it is important that these particular questions should be answered or problems explored; what other research is being or has been conducted in this area; and what particular contribution this particular project will make to the advancement of creativity, insights, knowledge and understanding in this area.
- It must specify the **research methods** for addressing and answering the research questions. You must state how, in the course of the research project, you are going to set about answering the questions that have been set, or exploring the matters to be explored. You should also explain the rationale for your chosen research methods and why you think they provide the most appropriate means by which to answer the research questions.

Research Question

We have discussed in earlier chapters the nature of research questions and the need to focus. ESRC Research Director Chris Caswill says that a problem with many proposals is that the topic is too broad. 'The topic itself must be researchable,' he points out. 'Sometimes it is such a large canvas that it is impossible to do.'

Janet Lewis, former Research Director of the Joseph Rowntree Foundation, concurs. Sometimes, the research question is not only vague, but even unimportant or boring: 'You can have really good science on a really boring topic,' she remarked, emphasising once again that the research question must match the funder's priorities.

Focusing on the research question is hard work, she admits, but it is critical:

> At one stage I started drawing up a kind of checklist of important points, and one of them is, if the background and elaboration of the problem is longer than the methods and the aims, then it goes in the bin. This is a slight exaggeration, but I think there is, more seriously, a drawback. There's the kind of focus of the issue – does it fit into the

priorities that we've identified? Have they addressed the issue? Quite a few people haven't really, because they're, not surprisingly, trying to make their interests fit ours because they're desperate for money, so they will slightly modify what they want to do to try to fit into our brief, and it may not work.

Context

The context referred to here is both the background of the research question and also the context of the funding partner and their community. We have already explored the need to understand who the partner is, who their stakeholders are and how you fit into that community and can enrich it. Now, in your proposal, is the time to articulate that and make it clear to the funder that not only have you taken the time and effort to find out, but know how to work within that context.

This book has referred to funders' guidance notes and websites. One of the interesting features of websites is that the owner can review and assess the navigation behaviour of those who visit it. Website owners review that kind of information frequently in an effort to improve their sites, but it is also used to get a better picture about the behaviour and characteristics of those who visit them.

Sharon Witherspoon, deputy director of the Nuffield Foundation, told administrators at a recent funding symposium that it is evident many researchers do not bother to find out enough about the organisation: 'we know because we can see how far they've gone into our website. Many people do not go far enough.' They do not, in other words, develop 'in-house scrutiny'.

How can you demonstrate in your proposal that you have taken the trouble to do that 'in-house scrutiny'? Some of your scrutiny will become obvious in the way that you frame your questions and situate them within the context. You can go further by using the actual language of the funder and referring to, for example, their strategic aims or points of ethos by quoting them directly. Don't just do the homework; be seen to be doing it.

Method

Although this point has been dealt with in earlier chapters, it is worth repeating here as it is so often given as the primary reason for application failure. Describe your method in as much detail as possible. This is obvious, and yet often overlooked by poorly considered proposals.

Asked for his 'top tips' for application success, Chris Caswill stressed that method is often the single most frequent cause of failure.

'These are applications to do research, so it is extremely important to discuss the research in the application,' he remarked, not without a hint of irony. Some applicants only offer a brief discussion of the subject area and a literature review. The methods must be appropriate and well-designed for the question, but simply mentioning that is not enough. Sufficient detail is necessary to convince the funder the methods have been designed and defined and the applicant knows how to carry them out. 'The majority of proposals which get close yet fail, do so because research methods are either inappropriate or ill-defined,' Chris says.

How can you be sure your proposal adequately covers method? A checklist of common methodology faults proposed by Janet Lewis, former Research Director of the Joseph Rowntree Foundation, may help:

- Vague research design and lack of clarity
- Poor information about methods of data collection
- Weak discussion of data analysis
- Unrealistic timescales, often related to under-budgeting.

If, for example, you are proposing a quantitative survey, say what it will look like. If you are going to conduct focus groups, say why and how you will analyse the findings.

'I think everyone wants to do focus groups these days,' she says. 'They may be very trendy, but they are difficult to do properly and analyse. Some people do not give enough background about this.'

Also, some experienced researchers assume that their experience alone will reassure the funder that they know how to collect and analyse data. Beware, she advises, of taking this for granted and ensure you articulate your approach in detail.

Sharon Witherspoon, elaborates this point by saying that some research proposals do not link types of aims with appropriate methods. The question, for example, may be numbers-based but the approach, in contrast, centres on qualitative methods.

The same advice applies to how much money you think you will need. Poor budgeting often results from poor consideration of method. Do you really think, for example, you can expect one research assistant to carry out six interviews a day for six months? Better to budget for two than appear that you have not understood the implications of your research methods.

Writing Style

Many proposals which are well-structured and considered fail to convey the key points. This often happens when people try to write in a more complicated and supposedly sophisticated style than is necessary. As one funder noted, 'when you read an application written in jargon you know it covers up messy thinking'.

It's hard to improve upon what George Orwell did to illustrate the importance of how clear language links to clear thinking. His advice is that if you don't know what to say, use as many syllables and vague words as possible. He offered an example from Ecclesiastes to make the point:

> I returned and saw under the sun, that the race is not to the swift, nor the battle to the strong, neither yet bread to the wise, nor yet riches to men of understanding, nor yet favour to men of skill; but time and chance happeneth to them all.

Few could say they don't get the author's point, but how clear would be the meaning if we read instead Orwell's own parody of how the passage would be written in 'modern English' (or, as we might say, 'academic English'):

> Objective considerations of contemporary phenomena compels the conclusion that success or failure in competitive activities exhibits no tendency to be commensurate with innate capacity, but that a considerable element of the unpredictable must be invariably taken into account (Orwell, 1957, pp. 149).

In describing what it is about, it is useful to bear in mind the standard checklist given for story-writing in primary school:

- Who
- What
- Where
- When
- Why
- How.

Try to keep your paragraphs short and use devices such as bullet points to break up the text.

It is also worth remembering that a picture may indeed paint a thousand words. Many funders and successful researchers recommend using diagrams. This can quickly capture and convey important information. Professor Rosalind Edwards at South Bank University, who is currently directing a five-year ESRC-funded programme on Families and Social Capital, says that her use of diagrams was one of the strengths of her proposal. She wanted to demonstrate that the programme would be well managed through a team structure which reflected the aims and objectives of the programme. This point is made by the ESRC in its guidance notes to applicants:

> Diagrams and other graphic devices are a very effective way to get across points and overcome language barriers. Employ them wherever possible. You might use a diagram to express the conceptual framework you are adopting, an organogram for the management structure, and a GANNT or PERT chart to describe the workplan.[1]

Check your proposal for grammar and spelling, letting other people read it so that the errors you can't see are spotted. As Peter Brown, Secretary of the British Academy remarked at a research funding symposium: 'Assessors take a dim view of illiterate applications'.

Finally, keep to the word length. If the funder asks for 200 words, do 200 and no more. Exceeding the recommended length is annoying for the funder because it makes it more difficult to compare proposals. It also reflects badly on the researcher who apparently is not thinking clearly enough. After all, it is harder to write 200 well-constructed and concise words than 800.

---

1   www.esrc.ac.uk/ESRCContent/researchfunding/

Talk to Them!

If you are uncertain about any aspect of the proposal, just ask. Readers will by now be familiar with this mantra running throughout this book: 'talk to them!' Janet Lewis mused about that:

> Sometimes I can't understand why they
> brought this to us because it's so obvious that
> they've not thought that one through. You
> have to think sometimes that people are
> sitting in their garret alone somewhere,
> writing, and that's not the way to develop a
> really good research proposal.

Elizabeth Atherton of Nirex says this is something applicants often overlook: 'They can ring up anytime during the tender process,' she stresses. This reflects the aims of the organisation itself, which is committed to transparency, she explains: 'We're not just transparent in terms of product but of process.'

The conversations may allow an applicant to deviate slightly from a standard specification by adding a note that more detail in one area needs to be explored. She advises people to:

> Put in a statement that x, y, or z can be met as
> expected, but request a meeting to discuss
> further. This shows respect, shows that
> you're listening. That's the added value, this
> shows how we could benefit further. It pushes
> the boundaries.

One successful researcher pointed out that academics may not ask for help because it isn't part of academic culture. Senior academics are, of course, expected to know everything. In his experience the best approach is to develop a rapport with people within the funding organisation:

> There is that grey area and you've got to
> know who you're dealing with. Don't send
> things anonymously. Find out who's involved
> in the process. Develop a contact, rapport –
> ask him, seek advice. Don't be too confident
> in your ideas. Everybody's got good ideas and
> try to learn from other people's experience. A
> lot of people prefer to have all of nothing

rather than half of something and that's a big problem because they're academics. You know, we traditionally don't like asking for help. I think that's a key point.

There is a view that if we just get on with the job and do our best we'll get ahead. Unfortunately, that is wrong. When we study who gets ahead quickly and who gets their projects approved, we find it is often the person with the best connections and who uses those connections to enrich their knowledge.

Internal Review

Peter Townsend, Research Manager in the Research Office at Loughborough University, emphasises the importance of internal review systems.

Once you have written your case for support, you need to stand back from it. Academics are close to their work and sometimes forget that this is not an academic paper, but a sales pitch. Often, this doesn't come across. Be responsive to their requirements; know the sponsors' regulations inside-out.

He points out that this requires a fine balance at times between complying with the regulations of the external sponsor and the academic's needs. Officers like his can help review proposals to see if they achieve that balance. In Chapter 7 and in this chapter we reviewed the role of research administrators as part of the research team and how important they are in helping not just review proposals for technicalities, but for all the above points as well.

Many academics underestimate the role and potential of university research administrators. Some refuse to admit that an administrator outside a subject area could possibly have anything useful to say about a proposal, ignoring the fact that such people see more proposals and more responses from funding agencies in an average day than most academics see in a year.

One administrator recently entertained a group which was meeting to discuss research funding with an amusing, if somewhat bizarre, story about an academic at her institution who came to the administration office to seek information about creating a budget for a proposal. The administrator read through the proposal and noticed that it said little about the research methodology. When she helpfully pointed out that funding agencies normally like to see discussion and detail about method, the academic rejoined, 'well, this is just the way we do research here and if the ESRC doesn't like it, tough.'

They didn't, of course.

Conclusion

In writing a proposal, bear in mind the three key points which the AHRB state clearly:

- The research question – have the applicants addressed the issue?
- The context – has the funding body's needs and wants been properly researched; has 'in-house scrutiny' been undertaken?
- The method – is it described in detail? Are the applicants being realistic?

Make sure your writing style is clear and as simple as possible. Use diagrams where appropriate. Make sure you check your grammar and spelling very carefully. You are presenting a communication document.

Try to engage with the funding body, to demonstrate that you have read and acted on their notes for guidance. Someone has spent a long time writing them. It is likely to be well received if you can show that you have responded to them.

Finally, be conscious of using your institution's internal review systems properly. Research administrators can be highly valued colleagues in the successful submissions of proposals to funding bodies.

14 PRESENTATIONS

Some funders, particularly in the corporate sector, ask prospective researchers to give a presentation of their proposal to a group of key decision-makers. This usually entails speaking for about 20 minutes and answering questions or having an informal discussion. For many academics, accustomed to lecturing for an hour or two, this may seem like familiar ground. In practice, they report that the experience is markedly different from the lecture hall and they need to prepare in different ways.

Firstly, the purpose of the presentation is not the same as the purpose of giving a lecture. Presentations are not just for imparting information but for targeting the right information to a specific group. Although your specific objectives may vary slightly from presentation to presentation, the purpose is the same: convince the funder to say yes.

A presentation is only one stage in the application process, but David Crowther, Head of Research at London Metropolitan University, put it in perspective by saying: 'You won't win on it but you can lose on it.' In other words, a good presentation cannot rescue a bad proposal, but a good proposal can be ruined by a bad presentation.

Why? Some people may resist the idea that their personal skills in presenting their work should matter so much – and for some work, they would be right. But, as we have seen so far in this book, many research projects emphasise the skills of collaboration and partnership. If that is the nature of your work, and particularly if you are asking someone to fund that work in a partnership arrangement, then part of your job will be to convince them that you are a worthwhile investment. You will have, on average, less than an hour to do so. Some professional presenters will say you have less than a minute, because most people form strong first impressions about people which take seconds to create and can last forever.

It may strike you as unfair that your excellent work and impeccable reputation should be threatened because someone doesn't like your look or your manner of speaking. Why, for example, should you dress any differently just because you are presenting to a group of managers in the private sector?

If you are proposing to work closely with a group of people over, say, a year or two, they will want to know if they can trust you. Your ability to put them at ease and, while not pretending that you are one of them, show that you can empathise with them will help relax them more than all the words on paper you will provide.

Jane Hunt, an experienced researcher from Lancaster University who works widely with the corporate sector, says that her aim is to reduce the fear many people have of academics and other so-called experts: 'Help them relax – they're often frightened of you!' She concentrates on translating complex theories, remembering that:

> you need to translate what is academically
> interesting to what is commercially useful.
> The big boss is going to read one sheet of
> paper. You may have to reduce your PhD to
> four bullet points.

Winning research funding through presentations means adapting your message to the needs of your audience. In this chapter, we will explore the skills of giving effective presentations with the specific aim of gaining an audience's:

● Interest
● Conviction
● Commitment
● Participation.

Preparing the Presentation

Be clear about why you are giving the presentation and how you will use the various benefits a presentation can bring.

In a presentation you can:

● interact with more, maybe all, decision-makers simultaneously
● involve your personality to make a human connection with your audience
● create impressions with visual images to bring life to your message
● ask questions and receive immediate feedback from your audience.

If you are unfamiliar with the media, it can be unnerving. We have all heard stories of people dropping their notes, forgetting what they're trying to say, 'drying up', nearly (or really!) fainting, and other such horror stories.

But none of that, not even the dread, is necessary. Ninety per cent of 'nerves' is due to lack of confidence. Lack of confidence usually correlates to lack of preparation. By working from the inside out, building in purpose and conviction from the first moment of preparation, you will calm your nerves and deliver your presentation crisis-free.

There are many different reasons for giving a presentation. Let's say that you have been working on a proposal for corporate funding and you need now to present to the board of directors. You are on the agenda for 45 minutes, with 15 minutes for your presentation and 30 more to answer questions and discuss.

For every minute of a delivered presentation at this level, allow one hour for preparation. Assuming you have your facts and figures to hand, that means you can prepare your presentation in two working days, if you do nothing else. This should give you an idea of the amount of time you must be willing to invest.

Build Interest

Think why you are giving a presentation. Why is this different from a written proposal? What do you really want from the presentation? What action do you want the board to take at the meeting?

Review who will be there and why. Ideally, arrange a briefing session with your main contact where you can learn about who is attending, what their main interests and concerns are and what you should cover. Use your knowledge of the group to clarify their different needs – they will not all be the same. The finance director brings a different perspective than the marketing director, who thinks about it differently from the human resource director, who has a different view than the operations director, and so on. Using your background knowledge, tease out the needs of the group. Think about key organisation concerns like risk, security, familiarity, novelty, efficiency, value and innovation. This is important not only to help you prepare, but also to help you manage the presentation as you deliver it and generate discussion.

Jane Hunt, a contract researcher in the area of public consultation, says she deliberately uses her knowledge of group behaviour to sort out who is who and how to work the room. Are most people deferring to one individual and waiting for him or her to take the lead? Is there someone who holds a powerful position but is not contributing to the discussion? How can you draw him or her out?

The First 30 Seconds

Your objective in the opening moment is to engage interest. First impressions are made in the opening sentences. Do not begin by boring them with your background and credentials; they will only want to validate those once they decide to form a relationship. Your cv can be presented in a folder and you can summarise the key points at a more critical point in the presentation. From the outset, you need to establish that you understand the problem they are facing. Don't open with the standard, 'hello my name is Mary and I'm really pleased to be here and I'm going to tell you all about my background and my idea.'

Focus on them. Your direction needs to be towards their organisation and their needs. Practise something direct, such as:

> Do you know exactly why some people want to do business with you and others do not? I think you will find it has little to do with your products and prices but a lot to do with how you manage complexity. Let me explain, during the next 15 minutes, how we can help you understand and respond to that dynamic.

The Next 30 Seconds

Now that they are wide-awake, continue to build their interest: You will do this most effectively by reassuring them that what you are about to say is credible. Use here the old adage about presentations: tell them what you're going to say, tell them, tell them what you told them. Build a 30-second summary of what they can expect for the rest of your presentation. Something like:

> I'll be explaining firstly why complexity is an issue for the industry, then I will share with you some examples of how other people have tried to manage it. In the latter part of our presentation, I will explain the method we have devised for understanding this in your particular organisation and I will summarise what we propose as the next steps. I hope then we can discuss in more detail how we might move forward.

During the presentation, you should be following the simple structure outlined above: build interest, conviction, commitment and participation.

Build Conviction

Throughout every section of the presentation you need to anticipate the unspoken questions and concerns of the audience. Explore the kinds of questions they are likely to ask before they ask them. Create an imaginary dialogue with the audience during the preparation period by posing the kinds of common questions they will ask:

● What (is the problem, is the method, is the institution ...)?
● Why (do we have the problem, has no one spotted it ...)?
● Who (will benefit from the project, will be involved, will need to know ...)?
● Where (does this issue occur, does the work happen, does the result matter most ...)?
● When (does the problem occur, does the research stop, does it finish, does the benefit accrue)?
● How (do other people approach the issue, will the research group proceed, much will it cost ...)?

Although you will not be able to cover everything, choose the parts now which impact most on your objectives. Do you need to convince them that you understand everything about their industry, or is it your aim to make that orientation part of the research project? Do you need them to have faith in your wider, more in-depth background, to reassure them that you can acquire the requisite knowledge quickly? How much do they need to know now about the detail of your method?

One of the most exciting aspects of research is its uncertainty. This is not, however, likely to be the most important priority for your funder. While many academics enjoy the difficulty and perplexity of a research problem, most funders are interested in how to simplify and solve it. A good way to prepare is to work through how, if accepting the project would involve risk, you intend to reduce that risk.

There are several ways you can achieve this. For example, if conducting such research projects is foreign to their culture, show them how they can be involved and monitor progress. If the project requires a long-term investment, you may be able to demonstrate how tangible benefits can be gained at specific milestones. You need here to remove all the obstacles to help them feel reassured.

It is important to present both the content of the proposal and the factors which will help build their conviction. This takes not only information about the project but also appropriate messages about how the partnership and collaboration can work.

Build Commitment

Now that you have built their conviction in what you can do and how you can do it, they need to feel a sense of commitment for what can be done – what people in the corporate sector often call 'buy-in'. Put yourself in their place. Show them how your idea or your project will satisfy their needs. Give them a working example. Tell them about it in tangible terms, not abstract. This is the time when they need to see the project as a working reality.

Show them how what you are doing fits with their immediate and long-term concerns. Remember the who, what, why, where, when, how.

Build Participation

Here, in your closing moments, you need to invite them to take action. Tell them what you want to happen next and ask for help. Tie this back to the outcomes you identified earlier and be specific. If you are asking for £50 000 to conduct this research over the next two years, do not say 'We need investment to take this forward'. Say, 'We need £50 000 over two years'. And say specifically why.

It is an old adage amongst salespeople that the main reason people don't 'win the business' is because they don't ask for it. It is sometimes tempting to end a presentation by lamely saying something like, 'Thank you for your time and I hope this interested you'. That is not normally the point of a presentation and it is not the point of your audience's attendance. They, like you, need to make decisions and act. Few people get paid just to think, or consider.

This is where some academics falter. It is not part of the academic culture to demand people's action. Universities are places where adults come voluntarily to learn and research; it is expected that commitment follows. This may be an unrealistic expectation to carry to a presentation. As one researcher says, 'I'm successful because I follow through. I don't leave a meeting without knowing what will happen next. I think it's called closing.'

Tell them what participation looks like. Pretend you're making a movie: if you were filming the 'participation scene', what would they actually be doing when they were participating? Writing a cheque? Hosting a seminar? Opening their files for you? Visualise it so it is clear, then spell it out.

Be specific about what exactly you want to happen. What would you like to happen now, and what can come later? Do you want them to give an instant answer? Would it be reasonable to accept a decision later? How much later? Will anything be open to negotiation? What? If you were giving a presentation to a client company, for example, an acceptable outcome might be to secure a meeting with one of their managers. At an internal board meeting, an acceptable outcome might not just be 'yes, go ahead' but 'meet with a sub-committee next week'.

Technical Points

Remember, your audience only wants the highlights, the key points. You can leave a longer report for digestion later if they're interested. But, if you send them to sleep during the first presentation, they won't ask for more.

Most presenters in the corporate and public sector use digital technology, most commonly Microsoft PowerPoint. This may pose a technological challenge for many academics. As one researcher said: 'If I need some help with using Word I just ask anyone, but no one knew how to help me with PowerPoint.'

PowerPoint is a Microsoft software program which allows you to create 'slide' effects, including animation, art, words and sound in a variety of styles and colour. When you have created your presentation, you will save it on a disk. If the people organising the venue know you will use PowerPoint, they will provide a computer and projection screen for you to use.

The same rules apply to PowerPoint as to any presentation using visual aids.

BE PREPARED

If you are using PowerPoint, make sure the venue is set up for you beforehand. Your host should arrange this, but check anyway. Establish whether you are bringing your own laptop or are using a computer in the presentation venue. For anything other than a presentation to two or three people (which can be done, albeit not very comfortably, around a PC screen) the computer will be connected to a projector which will project on to a screen or blank wall.

If you are bringing your presentation on disk, do make sure the disk has been properly virus-scanned! Bring a back-up disk as well, just in case your disk doesn't work for some reason. Arrive early, and make sure the system works. You will all have seen presenters at conferences struggling with trying to get a presentation working while the audience sits impatiently.

Many presenters bring a copy of their presentation as audience handouts. These are best done using the 'Print' menu and toggling the 'Print What' default from 'Slides' to 'Handouts'. Handouts can normally be printed three or six to a page. Create your slides in 24-point type or larger, so people can read your handouts.

KEEP IT SIMPLE

One experienced presenter has this to say about how some people use the technology: 'They're like kids with a toy, trying every available feature for no particular purpose. It's very annoying and distracting to watch – words in every type size possible come whizzing in from the side of the screen accompanied by strange noises.' A presentation needs above all to communicate, and to do so professionally. PowerPoint is fun the first time you use it and get to know its many features, but your audience have seen hundreds of presentations – they won't be impressed that you know how to use the 'dissolve' feature accompanied by a 'whoosh' sound.

SLOW DOWN

The purpose of the visual is to aid understanding, not confuse people. Design your presentation screen by screen and focus on main points. Use 24-point type so that people can see it easily.

DON'T READ

There is nothing more annoying in a presentation than watching a presenter's back as he or she methodically recites what you have already read in five seconds. For the same reason, try not to speak from a script. You should never read to people at a presentation – they could do that for themselves. All you need are key points to prompt you. Ideally, you will have your points written on small numbered cards with a hole punched in one corner and a tie keeping them together.

KEEP TO TIME LIMITS

It is likely that people have things to do other than being at your presentation.

They are making time. Do not overrun! It is disrespectful and shows disorganisation and under-preparation, neither of which are the impressions you want to give. If you have been asked to do a 15-minute presentation plus 30 minutes question and answer, that is because the 30 minutes has been judged as essential to gauge the partnership and relationship possibilities, and to allow those in the room to explore ideas or doubts. It is not an invitation to run to a 30-minute presentation instead so you can get more information in, in the hope of being more convincing. Their Q&A time is as important (or more important) than your presentation time.

DON'T FORCE-FEED YOUR AUDIENCE

You may know your proposal inside out and love it, but your audience does not. They will have a limited attention span. They cannot and normally will not be willing to take in a lot of information in a short time. Stick to your key points. Use one screen or slide for each key point you want to develop. If you have a 15-minute presentation slot, prepare *no more than* seven slides (talk to each one for two minutes, minimum). In a presentation, more is usually less.

NEVER BE, OR SEEM, UNDER-PREPARED

Do not apologise to an audience for not having had enough time to prepare properly because you have been 'too busy'. Don't say that you have really more information to put across than the allocated time allows. Don't put up a slide with a table or figures which no one can read then apologise for the fact that no one can read it. Don't be sorry for being late, or for losing your disk, or for not being able to make the projector work, or for misspellings.

REHEARSE

Then rehearse again.

All the same rules apply to a presentation on acetates. You still need to pre-arrange an OHP and screen, still need to arrive early and make sure it works; you may still want to bring handouts.

Answering – and Asking! – Questions

No one is expected to know everything. Part of how you will structure your presentation will be to forestall obvious questions and anticipate concerns. You should therefore be left with a question period which is more devoted to exploration than clarification. Questions like 'how many people will be involved' or 'when do we get results' should have been dealt with in your formal presentation.

Jane Hunt summarises this point succinctly: 'Think about how they will understand, access and use your work. Think one step ahead.'

The discussion period is not just an occasion for people to grill you about your detail; it is also an opportunity for you to talk to your potential partners. If you have been briefed on the event and know who is coming, you can prepare a few opening questions which will generate discussion.

Be brief and to the point in your reply – resist the urge to wander off the topic. After one question is answered, allow a pause or ask another question: don't let the silence force you to fill it with babble. Just answer any questions as best as you can. Don't be afraid to say, 'Good question. I don't know the answer right now, but it is something to think about.' Don't fake it. No one expects you to know it all. The important thing is to impress them sufficiently with your confidence. They'll then know that you're best placed to work out the uncertainties and put it all into practice.

Conclusion

'You won't win on [a presentation] but you can lose on it.' Successful researchers know that bids do not sell themselves. They need to be professionally and engagingly presented to an audience.

No presenter, however skilled, will be able to 'sell' a research proposal which doesn't fit. What you must be able to do, though, is to help your audience understand the key points (they will not have read the proposal as thoroughly as you have) and how they match their needs. The research partnership is a relationship – your audience want to feel that you and your team are people they can have a productive, trustworthy and mutually beneficial relationship with.

Help your audience relax – dress in the type of clothes they might wear for work, demonstrate that you understand their organisation, learn and use their names, and take care not to alienate them with jargon or acronyms.

Prepare your talk – rehearse what you are going to say. Don't overrun your allocated time.

Focus on them not on you – try to address their needs, not yours. Use 'you' or 'we' more than 'I' or 'my'.

Be clear – address who, what, where, when, why and how.

Reassure – point to tangible outputs and milestones where your funders can expect to see progress. They may not be as engaged with the uncertainty and excitement of research as you are. They are more likely to be interested in outcomes than the research process.

Be specific. Be clear on what outcome you would like from the presentation and ask for it. If you need £20 000 a year committed over three years, with £20 000 paid on commencement, don't hope your audience somehow figures that out. Ask for it.

Use appropriate technology. Increasingly, in a corporate setting, this will be a Microsoft PowerPoint (or equivalent) presentation. Prepare, and make sure it works.

Try to anticipate some likely questions. Avoid being defensive, or bluffing an answer – there is no harm in saying 'I don't know that, but I'll find out and get back to you tomorrow'.

A good presentation is in direct correlation to the amount of preparation you do. If you are prepared, that means you will be relaxed, empathetic with your audience, confident the technology works, and able to deal with most questions.

If you have prepared, done the best you can, and lose the funding to a different bid – so be it. You have done your best. If you have done a great research proposal and a sloppy, under-prepared presentation and lose the funding to a different bid – learn the lesson, and be sure to allow yourself more preparation time in future.

15 A WORD FROM YOUR SPONSORS

The moment arrives for an *intermezzo*, a term from Italian opera to describe the middle, lighter movement of a large composition. The purpose of this intermezzo is to open briefly a few doors into the world of funding agencies where, through their own words, we can detect the strains of humanity. Too many researchers, particularly inexperienced ones, do not recognise that behind the thick walls, heavy guidance books and sometimes formidable wording of application forms are people, just like us.

The following excerpts from various funding bodies should be read with the purpose of hearing the nuances in the language, and sensing the determination – and sometimes frustration – of the people who may one day be your partners.

A good example of just how much language matters is to look at the objectives set out in the description of the Local and Regional Government Research Programme within the Local and Regional Government Research Unit. Amongst the paragraphs referring to proposal criteria lies a short reference to 'the need to ensure relevance and vfm'.

Vfm? By now, of course, you should know that 'vfm' stands for value for money, but how much does the casual acronym tell us about this potential funder? That, perhaps, the concept of value for money is so deeply embedded, it can be left to an abbreviation. It is part of their language.

Stating the Obvious

A certain wistful tone creeps into the guidance notes given by the ESRC below, which suggests that too many applicants have not bothered with such basic advice as reading the guidance notes. Instead, they may take a rather perfunctory attitude to 'filling in' an application form, rather than see it as a masterpiece of relationship management:

> **Read the rules and the guidance notes**
> attached to the application form which are

> designed to help you through the 'filling in'
> process. This cannot be over-stressed;
> familiarising yourself with the content of the
> ESRC Research Funding Guidelines may
> seem tedious but will help you to avoid basic
> mistakes which at best will require
> clarification with office staff and at worst may
> prejudice chances of success. (Emphasis
> theirs, in this and all extracts in this section.)

Further advice is given on how to write proposals, ending with a sentence which suggests that weary assessors have had a few too many late nights struggling with poorly constructed proposals:

> do take the trouble to check spelling,
> grammar and punctuation. These are all part
> of the quality of presentation and
> **presentation matters!**

And then, just in case you didn't get it first time, make no mistake ...

> Get your proposal in on time. If you miss the
> deadline – even by a minute – it will be
> rejected. To be on the safe side, try to submit
> your proposal at least a week ahead of the
> deadline, using a courier.

Puzzled as to why your brilliant application was rejected? The ESRC explains why this might have been. It's obvious, of course:

> Commission staff will read your proposal to
> check that it meets the basic funding criteria.
> Has it been submitted on time? Does it meet
> the programme's objectives? Does it contain
> sufficient partners? The summary of your
> proposal will play an important part in
> helping them answer these questions. In FP4
> around 15 per cent of proposals were rejected
> at this stage. If you fall at this hurdle, your co-
> ordinator will be notified immediately.

No surprises here. Nothing hidden, nothing to trip you up or trick you. Remember, they want to give their money to good applicants! But to qualify as a good applicant, you have to jump some basic hurdles. Here's another one: the ESRC's advice on basic rules of organisation:

When the call is announced, you must obtain
from the Commission a copy of the relevant
information pack which will provide all the
necessary details and funding criteria, as well
as the application forms. Every partner
should read the documents thoroughly and
suggest appropriate alterations to the
proposal in the light of any changes to the
programme's objectives. These should be
taken into account in the co-ordinator's final
draft, which must be signed off by all the
partners.

Another example of having to state the obvious is given by the AHRB whose
first point about eligibility – and the entire premise of this book – couldn't be
clearer:

Your application will be considered eligible
for support if:
the research itself complies with the Board's
definition of research; and its subject matter
falls within the remit of the Board.

The need to match the funder's needs is also top of the list from the Joseph
Rowntree Foundation:

Full details of the Foundation's interests and
those of each Committee are given in the
Current Priorities section. When looking at
each proposal, the relevant Committee will
consider:

- the relevance of the topic to the
  Foundation's priorities;
- whether the work will offer new insights or
  developments;
- the soundness and appropriateness of how
  the work will be done (for research projects
  this covers both the research design, the
  methods and the analysis);
- whether partnerships with relevant
  organisations and service users are in place
  where these are important;
- the ability of the staff to carry out the work
  and complete on time;

- the likely policy and practice implications;
- a thorough approach to dissemination.

The British Academy also takes a rather pointed approach, both to eligibility and punctuality. Academics may like to work to last-minute deadlines, but the clear message here is that the Academy does not like to be rushed. It even highlights in bold, for those of you who didn't pay attention, who is eligible. Helpfully, it also suggests that people at different levels of academic status are eligible:

> Most awards are made to staff employed in universities and other institutions of higher education, but applicants are not restricted by either academic or employment status. Rather, they must show that they are seeking support for advanced research at postdoctoral or equivalent level. **PhD candidates are not eligible to apply**, whether or not the project is related to the topic of their thesis. Awards are not available for the support of courses of study leading to professional qualifications. Awards cannot be made retrospectively; applications must be made in time for them to be considered well before the research or other work to which they relate is due to begin.

In 20 Words or Less

When it comes to summarising basic requirements and critical success factors, the funding agencies take the short and sharp approach. Look at what the ESRC put in bold type for emphasis, to draw attention to how strongly they feel they must stress the obvious, like **correct** and **all** (Table 15.1). Pull it together, dear readers. Someone has let the side down badly here. Why do some of these checklists make us feel slightly childish, as if we're being reprimanded by a parent whose patience is coming to an end?

For those who missed the positive points the Joseph Rowntree Foundation offered about good proposals, Table 15.2 presents virtually the same points again to explain why proposals are rejected and what their common weaknesses are.

Table 15.1 ESRC Guidelines Checklist for Success

A Checklist for Success

Before you send off your application, make sure that it has all the ingredients for success. It must:

- be clear and concise to a non-native English speaker;
- address the objectives of the call and match the evaluation criteria;
- be original and scientifically excellent;
- have a group of complementary partners;
- demonstrate strong project management capacity;
- show commitment to exploiting and disseminating your results;
- include procedures for monitoring and evaluating the project;
- have realistic costs that are within the call's budget;
- include all required documentation and be signed.

Check the details – once you have completed the application form make sure that all the required information is provided. Some of the most common omissions and problem areas are:

- obtaining **all** the necessary signatures and institutional stamp (not required if submitting using the electronic form which must be despatched by registered despatchers in institutions);
- a covering letter in the case of resubmissions;
- omission of dates of birth for co-applicants or of cvs for named research staff;
- the equal opportunities form not completed for all named applicants and attached to the front of the **original only** (please check it has not been attached to any copies of the application);
- the **correct** number of copies (not required for applications submitted using the ESRC electronic form);
- a realistic start date;
- details of **previous/current applications** with reports on current projects or end-of-award reports where required. **We will not process** new applications if an end-of-award report is overdue;
- a proposal limited to **six pages** (or twelve in the case of applications over £400 000).

Source: www.esrc.ac.ik/ESRCContent/researchfunding/

The Medical Research Council demonstrates in its checklist (Table 15.3) how its criteria are consistent across its schemes. There are certain requirements, such as scientific rigour, your expertise and how your proposal

Table 15.2   Joseph Rowntree Foundation: common weaknesses

Some proposals are turned down because the Foundation cannot give the topic sufficient priority even though the proposal is well thought out and presented. But proposals are often rejected because insufficient information has been provided about key aspects or there is a lack of clarity about what is planned, and insufficient detail about methods to be used. For example:

- The proposal describes the background to the project at some length but gives very few details about aims and methods.
- The aims of the project are very vague or are couched in terms of the process, e.g., the aim of the project is to carry out a 'descriptive study of X' or a 'survey of Y'.
- The design of the study lacks clarity or robustness so that there is a mismatch between the issues being addressed and the approach adopted, or what is planned is over ambitious.
- Information about data collection is insufficiently detailed. If interviews are going to be carried out, it is important to give information about the number of interviews; how the sample would be selected; and the form in which the data would be collected. (Any proposal which talks in terms of 'some people will be interviewed' is unlikely to be funded).
- Details of the way the data will be recorded and analysed are lacking. This is particularly the case where the use of focus groups is proposed.
- Information about the proposer's own knowledge and skills is lacking. In addition to the standard information provided on a CV, it is helpful to have a short summary – two or three sentences – of the experience that members of the team carrying out the work have had using the methods being proposed.
- Timescales and staff resources are unrealistic or inappropriate. This includes too much work being planned for the time available, or too much of the field work and analysis being left to inexperienced research staff.
- It is unclear how the proposed outputs could be derived from the material.

Source: www.jrf.org.uk/funding/applyforfunding/good.asp

matches the council's objectives, that are simply not negotiable. While this may all sound strict and a little forbidding, pay attention to the last line, again in bold type just in case you weren't sure. It is also interesting to see how two of the points about your track record and history correspond with similar points in the Joseph Rowntree Foundation list.

Beyond the obvious 'summary' section there are other hints and clues the diligent researcher can find. It is worth checking funders' websites for similar checklists. Information given in other sections may be equally useful and

Table 15.3 Medical Research Council advice to applicants

Assessors will ask questions such as:

First and foremost – what is the scientific quality of your proposal?
Do you have the necessary expertise and commitment?
What is the significance of your topic and what potential does it hold to help improve human health or relieve the burden of disease?
Is your strategy coherent and is it relevant to the MRC's strategy?
Was your previous research productive – did you meet your objectives?
Is your proposed research timely?
Are your aims and objectives realistic within the proposed time and resources?
Is the research environment suitable for your proposed study?
Are the type of support and management arrangements suitable?
Will the proposal provide value for money, taking into account NHS as well as MRC costs?
What are the ethical implications of your proposal?
Have you made arrangements to disseminate your results to potential users and to promote public understanding of science and commercial exploitation, as appropriate?

An informal chat is always helpful and office staff will be pleased to offer advice.

Source: www.mrc.ac.uk

serve as a summary. The AHRB, for example, in discussing the peer review process, offers several useful points:

> The peer reviewers will assess the proposal on the basis of its academic merit, taking into account:
>
> ● The significance and importance of the project, and of the contribution it will make, if successful, to enhancing or developing creativity, insights, knowledge or understanding of the area to be studied
> ● The appropriateness, effectiveness and feasibility of the proposed methodology, and the likelihood that it will produce the proposed outcome in the proposed timescale

- The ability of the applicant(s) to bring the project to fruition, as evidenced not only in the application itself, but in their previous track record, taking account of their 'academic age'
- Value for money, and in particular the relationship between the funds that are sought and the significance and quality of the projected outcome of the research.

That extract provides a wealth of information to embed into a proposal. How often in designing and writing a proposal do you take care to incorporate the language of the sponsor?

Remember, They're Human ...

From the ESRC guidelines:

> **If you are successful** after all the hard work, planning and nail-biting, then congratulations, and we hope the work proceeds without too many problems.

Your Institutional Sponsors

The future direction of funding is heavily influenced by the stance universities take. It is worth looking into your particular institution's strategy towards supporting research. As funding bodies become more aligned through, for example, Research Councils UK, so have universities through organisations like Universities UK,[1] formerly the Committee of Vice-Chancellors and Principals (CVCP). Here is what they see as their official position on funding:

> Universities UK has developed a plan of action for the coming three years, based on certain key assumptions about the political, fiscal, social and economic environment in the UK and abroad. We expect a UK general election within the first year of the plan, and elections in Scotland and Wales in 2003.

---

1   www.universitiesuk.ac.uk

Public and private funding will remain essential components of university funding, although the balance between the two may alter. Partnerships with a diverse range of private funders continue to flourish and increase in number. We expect increasing competition between universities nationally and globally, but also more opportunities for collaboration and strategic partnerships both within the UK and internationally. We look forward to working with all our partners to achieve these goals.

Strategic goal 1   Enlightened and enlightening: supporting high quality teaching and learning.
Strategic goal 2   Encouraging enterprise: promoting UK research and competitiveness.
Strategic goal 3   Opportunities for everyone: encouraging wider participation and social inclusion.
Strategic goal 4   Focusing on funding: improving funding for institutions and students.

Researchers might take heed of how Universities UK describe projects with 'partners':

These projects involve two or more organisations who are working to achieve a mutually beneficial end that they could not achieve by themselves.

Such a definition fits well with the theme of partnership and relationships running throughout this book. For Universities UK, current partners include The Association for University Research and Industry Links (AURIL), the Department of Trade and Industry (DTI) Innovation Unit and the Higher Education Funding Council for England SCOP (Standing Conference of Principals).

Your National Sponsors

This book began with an overview of the importance of research for enriching people's lives. It is, ultimately, to the British and European parliaments in Westminster and Brussels that researchers can look for guidance on strategic priorities. The Office of Science and Technology, with the Department of Trade and Industry, frequently issues reports and statements which indicate the research agenda. In December 2001, for example, a strategic statement called 'Forward Look' was issued[2] which provides rich detail and clues about the future of funding. Lord Sainsbury, Minister for Science, clearly stated these priorities:

> The 21st century promises to be even more exciting than the last as far as science and technology are concerned. We are set to see breakthroughs in areas like genome research and sustainable development that have the potential to bring improvements to our lives. But for this to happen, we need to see the output from scientific research successfully harnessed in innovative products and services. We also need society to be receptive to new technologies and to be confident that science is serving their best interests.

> These three elements – excellence in science, opportunities for innovation and confident consumers – were identified as this Government's priorities in the Science and Innovation White Paper, 'Excellence and Opportunity: a science and innovation policy for the 21st century' published in July 2000. The White Paper sets out the actions we are taking, and intend to take, to build on the UK's excellent record of scientific achievement, and to transform ideas and knowledge flowing from our science and engineering base into innovations that will improve the economic and social well-being of the nation.

It is the business of researchers to understand those priorities.

---

2   www.dti.gov.uk/ost/forwardlook01/

16 HOW PROPOSALS ARE ASSESSED AND CHOSEN

What Happens Next?

Most funding applicants wait until the last minute before sending in their proposal. As one funder noted, they receive 80 to 85 per cent of proposals on the day of the deadline. While deadlines are useful to focus people's attention, too often people wait until the last minute and therefore do not allow adequate time for both preparation and review.

The problem often occurs through not managing the internal review process, as discussed in earlier chapters. Research administrators can provide useful guidance, and several funding agencies are becoming more insistent that they are involved, particularly at the early planning stages, so that their experience and advice can be incorporated from the outset.

The ESRC, for example, has recently contacted universities to ask that systems are in place to allow all applications to be reviewed. Some research project managers I talked to say that they are starting to establish non-negotiable deadlines for proposals to be reviewed. The all too common practice of asking the research office to respond to requests for budget information or final signatures on a few hours' notice may in some cases come to an end.

One university research officer I spoke to, who remains anonymous by request, found that after the university instituted a stringent internal review process the number of proposals which were eventually submitted fell, but the success rate improved dramatically. As with so many other things, quality not quantity counts.

Rather than let your proposal be amongst many in the pile on the last day, think about giving your funder the opportunity to look at your work a little differently. There is no evidence that getting your proposal in a week early means it is more likely to be accepted, but common sense suggests that in some cases it might skew the assessment in your favour, however slightly.

This would particularly be true for organisations whose front-line staff are actively engaged in the filtering process.

Perhaps just as importantly, it should become part of your discipline to respect the funding relationship. How do you feel about getting all your student's assignments in on the same afternoon? Isn't it just that much nicer to have a few days' breathing space? How would you look on someone who rushes breathlessly into your office at two minutes to five on the final day, brandishing their just-completed work? Think this one through carefully in terms of deciding what kind of partner you want to be – someone who rushes through their work or someone who plans it carefully and strategically. However finely you want to shave the margin, the impression people have about you is a lasting one.

Managing the Review Process

Review methods change from funder to funder, as does the requirement to send in one's own set of references. These are sometimes called 'external assessors' and will either be sent directly by the applicant or contacted by the funder. It is important to manage this part of the cycle. Choosing the right referee is vital. In some cases they can be from the applying institution, and in other cases the application procedures specify that they should not. Read the documentation carefully! In all cases, funders ask that the reference should be about the applicant's research and academic ability, not personal characteristics.

It is important to inform your prospective reviewers about your research. If you do not, you risk an inappropriate or over-generalised comment (or, in some cases, a refusal to comment at all). Do not depend on your referee to remember deadlines, however well-intentioned they may be. Make sure you remind them.

The funder will usually choose from your reviewers and from their own list. This leads some researchers to fear that a particular reviewer may give them a bad review through poor past relationships. What if you do not get along with a particular expert in your field, or for some reason you have argued or vehemently disagreed with each other? The academic community in any one research area is relatively small and many people feel worried that the 'wrong' reviewer might condemn their proposals out of spite.

However, despite any mythology in this area, it is important to reassure researchers, particularly younger ones, that such bad reviews are rare, and are usually easily recognised. 'The green ink letters are fairly obvious,' said the Nuffield Foundation's Sharon Witherspoon. 'The more heated adjectives there are in the letter the more we'll think about getting a new reviewer.'

I also heard concerns that an unscrupulous reviewer might recommend the proposal is rejected but then will secretly use it for their own work. One funder described this fear as 'paranoia'. I certainly found no basis of truth in it, and it is usually only something about which inexperienced researchers worry.

Balance

How the reviewers assess your application will vary according to the funder's criteria. As the ESRC says in its guidance notes about EC programmes: 'Independent assessors, who will be experts in their field, will meet to evaluate your proposals. They will comment on its academic content, the quality of the management, the level of collaboration, and all the other "criteria for success" mentioned earlier.' An important point here is to note the ESRC's emphasis on collaboration. This is not likely to be a factor for being funded by the British Academy to do a post-doctoral fellowship, for example. The review process is always unique to the funder and, often, the scheme.

Final selection will, again, vary according to the funder's policies and priorities. Some, for example, may take final judgement based on maintaining a balanced portfolio of researchers. In the words of one programme director: 'Whittling through 350 proposals is exhausting and time-consuming. The short list of 50 was all alpha level. What made the difference then was balance.'

Balance across a portfolio of funded projects could mean a regional spread. Some funders would not want to see all their researchers based in a certain corner of the country or single institution. For a large programme, the balance will be a range and representation of disciplines with an inter-disciplinary mix. The funder's needs for balance can be determined by exploring their assessment criteria at the pre-proposal stage and emphasising your own particularities.

Another selection criterion may be the urgency to the funder of any particular piece of research. The EC, for example, is interested more in solutions and policy impact than theoretical undertakings, and therefore would select equally-graded proposals according to those criteria. The ESRC's guidelines on EC programmes imply a balance *within* the proposal of academic content, management quality and collaborative effort, suggesting that *all* these need to be present and strong in a balanced submission. The AHRB do not look for regional or disciplinary balance on principle. They emphasise that each proposal is judged on its own merits.

Feedback and Resubmissions

Sometimes, however hard you have tried, there is just not enough money to go round. The ESRC, for example, explains in its guidance notes that a rejected alpha-graded proposal means that although your proposal may be one the ESRC wanted to support 'in principle', there was just not enough money. Two-thirds of alpha-graded proposals are rejected for that reason. The ESRC also emphasises that researchers should not assume that just because their proposal was alpha level that they should consider resubmitting 'with some window-dressing adjustments'. Resubmissions are not encouraged unless it can be shown that the proposal has been significantly revised. Before you consider taking those steps, talk to them.

If, on the other hand your proposal was rejected with a beta grade, they do not advise any resubmission. They may offer reviewer comments but this is not given as an invitation to revise and resubmit.

The AHRB's Guidance Notes describe its assessments as falling into five potential categories as in Table 16.1.

Table 16.1 AHRB Guidance Notes on Grading

A+	An application of the highest quality: to be funded as a matter of top priority
A	An application of high quality: to be funded as a matter of priority
A–	A good application, fully worthy of funding
B	A good quality application, which is potentially fundable, but where there are significant reservations about either the framing or planning of the proposed research programme, the roles and responsibilities of those who will conduct it, or their readiness to conduct it, which need to be addressed before a higher grade can be awarded. The applicant is permitted to resubmit the application addressing the Board's concerns
R	An application not recommended for support and one which should not be resubmitted to the same AHRB scheme.

Source: www.ahrb.ac.uk/

It is apparent, therefore that potential for resubmissions varies considerably from funder to funder. Some do not allow any, while others will give feedback and engage with the researchers about revising. Other funders, such as the Nuffield Foundation, may accept short outline proposals so that the assessment can initially be swift. In practice, about 40 per cent are turned away as ineligible.

The drawback of outline proposals, as Janet Lewis, former Research Director of the Joseph Rowntree Foundation described, is that it often takes a full proposal to see whether negotiations will be worthwhile:

> We did try that at one stage and didn't find it terribly helpful, partly because the outline is just saying would you be interested in something on this sort of topic? The answer is, yes, we know that. Whether we'll fund it or not and get involved is in the detail of how you want to do it, which will be in the proposal not an outline.

For Professor David Crowther, head of research at London Metropolitan University, asking for feedback is essential whether or not resubmissions are allowed. The opportunity for feedback and resubmissions will vary according to the funder and the way they organise their assessment process.

> I've had as many failed bids as I've had successful bids, so I always ask for feedback about what was good and what was bad, because that helps to understand how you need to structure a bid for the future for that organisation.

Degrees of feedback and opportunities for negotiation will, as always, depend on the funder and its approach to relationships, but it is something that a researcher can look for throughout the proposal process. It is also one more reason to see the relationship as continuing rather than simply a one-off transaction. Just receiving a blanket yes or no does not offer room for collaboration. The researchers who conduct their funding relationships with the kind of integrity that allows the funder to invest in them first and negotiate later are, as one funder put it, those that they want to work with repeatedly.

David Crowther reinforces this:

Sometimes I've had help from the assessing panel, for example about our proposed methodology, and we've had feedback saying – wouldn't it be better to go about things in a different order, or do something slightly different, and that's been very helpful. Very often, that happens and the result is, they ask for you to resubmit your proposal along the lines that we've talked about, and we'll receive it much more favourably. Sometimes that happens, sometimes it doesn't. I think it's more likely to happen when you know the organisation and have some kind of rapport with the organisation. That rapport for me comes in part from successful bids, in part from bidding and being unsuccessful, because your name starts to be known.

If you know the funder and have that kind of rapport, it may be possible to discuss the resubmission face to face. In one researcher's experience, the best case is to be able to have a post-proposal interview with the prospective funder and discuss the detail and offer alternatives. In one particular case for example, the funder was clear that the proposal had too many stages and could not be achieved within the budget, but if a stage was cut then the project could go ahead on the basis of a resubmission: 'when they say please resubmit, what they're saying is, you do what we discussed and we'll give it to you.'

That may sound more like ultimatum than negotiation but, as always, this varies from funder to funder. It will then be up to the researcher to decide whether, as in the above example, that stage could be cut and preserve academic integrity or whether the concept of academic integrity itself needs to be negotiated. No research proposal can be perfect due to the uncertain nature of the research process itself. Sometimes, the negotiation phase gives the proper opportunity to revisit the process.

None of this will happen unless the researcher is open to the idea of partnership. During the course of researching this book, the stories about academic arrogance far outnumbered those about academic openness. One researcher described this kind of arrogance with an example about negotiating a large government contract:

The [Government] department sent a request for some information in a particular area. I

> think there were about 15 key academics who they identified. When I asked them why did I get the contract they said, well, out of the 15 e-mails we sent, 14 of them said go and buy my book, go and read my paper, except your e-mail which said come down and let's sit and talk about the issues. So, they came, sat, talked, and were impressed and the project itself then unfolded.

Being open to rejection or revision means being open to change. The more you can practise talking with potential funders and renegotiating proposals, the more likely it is you will be regarded as self-confident rather than arrogant.

The Worst That Can Happen

The worst scenario following any submission of a research proposal is not, as some may assume, rejection. The worst case is giving up. Of all the advice she can possibly give to researchers, Professor Rosalind Edwards at South Bank University says the most important is the most basic: never give up. She is currently directing a five-year ESRC Research Group on Families and Social Capital. It took her years of both success and failure to be in that position. Her principle was never to stop trying and never stop learning.

Look at your 'failed' proposal and review the options. If you did not receive feedback from the funder, ask. This will help you refine the current proposal, if that's what you need to do, or at least to become better at proposal writing for the next time. Sometimes, you can amend your proposal to suit a different funder and submit it to them.

It should, by now, go without saying that amending it involves taking all the steps previously explored in this book to get it right for a new target audience. You can also put it aside for months or longer and then review it again. As Ros Edwards pointed out to me, research priorities amongst funders change. It may just be the right proposal at the wrong time.

Conclusion

Busy people often prioritise by the most imminent deadline. But leaving submission of your research proposal until the last minute might prejudice your chances of acceptance. You may not get the most out of your internal review process with your research administration office. And, since most other applicants will be leaving submission until the last minute too, you may find that it is in danger of getting lost in the last minute submissions pile.

When using external referees for your submission, make sure you tell them what the research is about. This will help them produce references which are relevant to the research.

Projects are likely to be selected by a funding body using the concept of *balance*. This may be balance across a portfolio of projects to give regional or disciplinary representation, or on internal balance within an application of academic content, quality of management and quality of collaboration. You can make the balance concept work for you by understanding what a funding body is seeking to do, and noting carefully the criteria asked for in projects.

Try to get feedback to enable you to revise and resubmit, if necessary, either to the same funder or to a different one. If you can discuss and negotiate feedback face to face, so much the better. That's a real partnership.

Finally, if rejected, don't give up. Learn from the rejection, get your feedback, and try again!

PART IV

MAINTAINING THE RESEARCH PARTNERSHIP

17 MANAGING THE RESEARCH PARTNERSHIP

Relationships need care and attention. Funding partnerships can either grow or be allowed to wither away. The difference usually depends on how the researcher manages it. Why should researchers bother? Why is it important that the partner gains from the relationship in more ways than just receiving an end-of-project report?

This will depend on the researcher's objectives, but most researchers who have enduring relationships with funders find that these relationships are valuable. A good relationship makes for a more congenial research process in many cases, and will often make the difference between a good and bad evaluation, and the eagerness of the funder to work with the researcher again. Researchers who feel they have maintained good relationships are in no doubt that an effort has been needed from both parties. Here are some of the things that they do.

Communication

There are three critical success factors for ensuring relationships proceed positively: communication, communication and communication. Operate on the theory that the last thing a funder wants is to be surprised, and assume the responsibility to keep them informed and engaged. This is particularly important because research, by its nature, will change direction and emphasis.

It's something a programme director with the ESRC knew when he described his strategy: 'It's a matter of knowing their needs,' he said. 'I think of it as satisfying the office. Keep them informed. It's giving them lots of paper work, nicely presented, thickly bound, lots of detail.'

Keeping in touch with your funder is good advice. It will help prepare them for occasions when research changes or runs into difficulty. It is not the change itself that is likely to cause difficulty, but rather the way the situation is handled. Few people resist change per se. We may resist a change which involves losing our jobs, offices, status or plans for the future, but what we are resisting there is not change, but loss. It's important to identify what it is that you, the researcher, and the funder may lose or be worried about losing as the result of changes. It is unlikely that this will centre on a fear of change itself.

Researchers sometimes mistakenly assume that the funder will resist changes to the project and therefore should be kept in the dark as long as possible, with the final, different results somehow fudged in the hope that no one notices. The peer review process at the project's conclusion does not mean that the project has to replicate exactly its intentions if those changed during the course of the work. Sometimes that happens.

Dealing with Changes Arising in Research

'We do research', as one researcher put it, 'because we don't know what to do.' By definition this is a voyage of discovery. Everyone recognises that details may change during a project as more information and learning is acquired. Just because you did the research differently does not necessarily mean you did it badly. But how is anyone to know that? How will you manage those changes? Not managing them may result in you looking like you can't be trusted with research money.

An anthropology professor at a leading university told the story of a researcher who was funded to study gender issues in an Asian country, but realised after a few weeks on the ground that what she assumed was a working knowledge of the language was deeply inadequate to grasp the nuances of indigenous belief. Her only option was to cut her losses, retreat back to England and offer a more distant anthropological analysis with a more in-depth critical literature review than originally intended. This led the professor to conclude that although different than originally conceived, it was a good piece of work.

A funding director at a foundation recalls a similar incident, with a research team hoping to conduct in-depth research on homeless teenagers. They had been assured by a local charity that they would be granted access to the young people, but as the project began the relationship changed and the researchers were not given the access they had been promised. At this point, the research project finished early with an expanded literature review. Everyone was disappointed, but because the research team kept the funder fully informed, they emerged with reputation and credibility intact.

A female academic funded by the British Academy had her research influenced by more joyful circumstances – pregnancy. In this case, she described the Academy as understanding and supportive, allowing her to change her timing to account for her changed circumstances. Another British Academy researcher described how his project was temporarily put on hold – or 'intermitted' in funding jargon – because another funder wanted to back a particular aspect of his research which demanded urgent attention.

The purpose of these examples is to emphasise that what matters is not that the research changes but rather how the researcher will manage them in light of the final evaluation. The most important move is to involve the funder at key stages, not simply when they have asked for a report. Anticipate the response you are likely to receive if the end-of-award report comments that you varied considerably from the original brief. One way to avoid that is to keep the funder in the picture. All your correspondence will be kept in the file with your original proposal so that peer reviewers examining the evidence are able to see what happened and why.

The initiative for doing this lies with the researcher. It means sending in unprompted reports and making phone calls, backed up by correspondence, to keep the funder involved. Some will, at a stage where the research is changing, offer feedback. Others will simply say 'fine, go ahead' and some will want to argue against the change. In any case, it is during the course of the research that the intervention is necessary.

Some funding bodies have specific mechanisms to track changes. There may be advisory councils who meet with researchers regularly, or at least receive their reports. There may be more formal checkpoints, as with most EU projects, where the research is reviewed in detail every year. The role of project advisory groups also varies, depending on the funder. Some may exist to keep the research team accountable – to talk about reports, outcomes and dissemination and what to do next. Other groups will act much more as advisors and people to whom you can bring problems and agree modifications.

Feedback

This makes it more important than ever that researchers know in advance how the funder works. Dr Zahir Irani, of Brunel University, has broad experience of different sorts of funding relationships. Within European Community projects, for example, he acts as a reviewer and may see researchers twice a year. This is to ensure that money is being spent appropriately, deliverables that were originally planned for are being achieved and the project is kept on track. If the project is not running according to plan, the group will review why certain milestones aren't being achieved, what collective action has been taken to get the project back on time, and what will happen next.

The decision of the reviewers is then to agree whether to 'green flag' it, which means everything is OK; to 'amber' it, which is when they raise an issue of concern and address the actions to be taken for the deliverables to be back on target; or to 'red flag' it, which is saying they are not happy with the way that the money is being spent. At that stage, the commission will take appropriate action, which may end up being a form of legal action to recover monies. He observes that this is a completely different way of governing the spending of funds from, say, a small research council grant: 'It's a very different model, but then again you're talking about significantly large amounts of money.'

Some of Zahir's own funded projects have been supported by the UK government, others by the military and others by private industry. His involvement in the projects have ranged from being the sole investigator to others where he was leading a team of investigators and those where he was part of a team being led by others, both within the UK and Europe. His conclusion is that there is little which can be universally applied about managing those relationships, apart from the advice that 'when you seek your funding, you have to be very clear in terms of what mechanisms there are for feedback and communicating with the collaborators.' These, he emphasises, 'vary quite considerably'.

This means that the onus rests more with the researcher than the agency, which may take its processes for granted. Even if they are happy to not communicate with the researcher, his advice is for the researcher to communicate with them nonetheless. Being left alone may seem fine if you are a conscientious strategic planner and can follow your plans, but:

> It doesn't necessarily mean you'll stick to them because research never goes according to plan, so you have all sorts of problems in ensuring that you stick to those plans and having no accountability throughout the project life cycle really doesn't do you any favours, to be quite honest.

What is a researcher to do, then, without real feedback mechanisms until the final report? The problem is of self-management and deliberate strategies to communicate when none formally exists. This applies equally to the private and the public sector.

In her experience, Jane Hunt from Lancaster University finds that it may not be easy to get feedback from the funder. 'You have to work at this as many will not bother with feedback. You need to go and get it because feedback will influence evaluation and routes into the next project.'

Jane observes that some funders will welcome informal feedback throughout the project, but they may not know how to manage what they learn. Particularly in the private sector there may not be the language or framework to deal with changing issues. What academics call 'an interesting problem' they just call a problem. For most managers, problems are bad. Jane advises that if things start to go differently, the researcher should endeavour to go to the funder with solutions, not problems.

'It's how you present the issue,' she notes.

Nurturing Relationships

Ideally, every researcher has a personal, one-to-one relationship with someone inside the funding body who can support the research team through its vicissitudes. This rarely happens on large publicly-funded projects, primarily because the personnel change frequently. Keeping track of people within sections may be difficult. As one researcher observed: 'If you're moving people round every three years and the project lasts two to three years, then you're almost certainly going to find that the person you started with is now an ex-client.'

That doesn't mean there are not opportunities for relationships. Most researchers report that funding agencies are amenable and open to enquiries and discussions. This often comes as a surprise: 'Just talk to us' is a common piece of advice to potential and practising researchers.

Within some funding agencies, keeping people in the agency's office close to the researchers is not an accident but a matter of policy. While some agencies place decision-making away from the office and in the hands of peer reviewers, others prefer to develop their staff to qualify them for the initial stages of review. They will sometimes take decisions independently and sometimes with external advice, although final decisions will be taken by a committee composed of internal and external experts.

Within the private sector, the relationship is often more direct and centred on an individual. As Phil Macnaghten from the Centre for the Study of Environmental Change at Lancaster University (CSEC), describes his relationship with Unilever, a good working relationship can be a mix of formal and informal: 'I think we were both quite keen not to load up the relationship with too much bureaucracy, so it was slightly ad hoc.' Formal proposals and presentations were preceded by informal discussion.

> I mean, that's one of the beauties of this type of relationship. If it's set up right, with the people who matter, the quality of the relationship is the most important thing. If there's a track record, then it's often a phone call saying, we're thinking about this idea and what do you think about this, and what do you think you might be able to do, and then you put together a proposal and work it out …

Once the relationship is firmly established, the initiative for future work comes from both directions – some prompted by the researcher and others by the agency.

Reciprocity

It's not always a future contract that motivates communication within the partnership. An organisation with whom you have a relationship can be helpful in many, non-monetary ways. A relationship means that there is an expectation of reciprocity. Professor Mohamed Zairi, Director of the European Centre for Total Quality Management at Bradford University, for example, tells the story of needing to learn more about the operational logistics of the aviation industry to complement his knowledge. He went to an airline for which he had done research in a different area and explained his need. The airline agreed to give him access to planes and airports all over the world in exchange for sharing his findings.

'Giving something back' is one of Mohamed's aims in all his research partnerships. It's important to remember that this is an exchange relationship, he reminds us, not one where one partner takes money from the other and gives back a minimum of research.

Conclusion

Relationships are about reciprocity – about spending time and effort giving and taking things of benefit, and seeking mutual benefits. And like all relationships, a funder–researcher relationship is not fixed and static – it needs to be able to change and grow over time.

Because, however well-planned a project is, change is inevitable. We undertake research 'because we don't know what to do', in the words of one researcher. Changes to planned or expected outcomes and processes is inevitable.

Communication is vital in a project when these inevitable changes are unfolding. With communication, a relationship is nurtured and trust developed. Being clear about expected levels and forms of communication and feedback is vital. If the funding body does not make these clear, suggest something you feel is appropriate as a communication pattern: a month-end report, a meeting over lunch once a quarter, whatever will nurture the relationship. For with the relationship should come goodwill, good references, and, possibly, repeat projects.

A good working relationship is likely to be a mixture of formal and informal, professional and personal. For a relationship to be real, both parties need to be conscious of what they are giving, not just what they are taking. Taking a funder's money in return for delivery to specification is a minimum expected contractual obligation. Try to see how to go beyond that. The next chapter explores this point further.

18 MONITORING AND EVALUATION

The monitoring and evaluation process begins long before the research starts. Arguably, it begins when you select your funding partner.

It would be a mistake to assume that nothing need happen until the award's end, when peer reviewers will look at your project and assess whether it met its objectives. That seems, on the surface, to be a simple matter of filling out a form and ticking a box which shows that your finished work lines up against the proposal. But this, say many researchers, is only half the story. It is what might be called a necessary but insufficient condition of maintaining research partnerships.

What funders really need to see is how you added value to either the larger research programme in which you were engaged, or to the academic community as a whole. This not only gives them a way to measure how their money was spent, but it allows them to review its future spending and priorities. Knowing this makes the difference between what is necessary to satisfy the funder's long-term objectives and what meets their immediate needs. People who aim to be in research relationships long term need to gain a reputation for doing more than the minimum. This chapter addresses two important questions:

1   How are you ensuring that the funder knows you delivered what you said you would?
2   How are you ensuring that the funder knows you are delivering value to affect not only your immediate project but also future research?

Delivering What You Promised

Projects will be monitored and evaluated differently, according to the funder. Their process and criteria is something the researcher needs to establish long before submitting a proposal. How it occurs will define whether the project is judged a success and is therefore an important variable to identify and manage. A golden rule about any kind of evaluation is to know and, if possible, influence the criteria for success.

This does not mean that you have to arrive at startling conclusions or offer unique evidence. It just means you have to do well what you said you would do and articulate the benefits. It is what adds to the pleasure in reading a good final report, reflects Janet Lewis, former Research Director of the Joseph Rowntree Foundation:

> Essentially, I think the real stars are the ones that find really interesting things. But, if it's a nice piece of research, I feel really pleased even if they haven't found hugely exciting things. If the appropriate methods have been used and the conclusions are reasonable enough to address the things that they want to address, then I think, well that's really good.

Within a funding body, monitoring and evaluation processes will vary depending on the size and nature of the project. But that does not need to lead to any confusion on the researcher's part as to what is important. As Steve Morgan, the AHRB's Head of Corporate Projects and Evaluation, explains, the common thread is 'have you delivered what you were funded to deliver?' That is, at the bare minimum, the formal, contractual arrangement.

Within the AHRB, some awards in specific schemes, and all awards over £100 000, are reviewed annually via an annual monitoring form. All awards are peer-reviewed at their conclusion to assess how the aims and objectives have been met and how specific outputs have been created. If, for example, the award was to fund a book, has the book appeared? If it was to fund a production, has that happened? This is a process-driven review where the main question is: have you delivered what you were funded to deliver?

An ESRC-funded project led by Professor Rod Rhodes in the Department of Politics at the University of Newcastle, which we discussed briefly earlier, was praised in just those terms. The programme – Whitehall, The Changing Nature of Central Government in Britain – ran between 1995 and 1999 and comprised 23 projects in two phases. One reviewer had this to say in terms of value:

> The volume of research produced under the Whitehall Programme and the number of research reports (papers, articles, and books) already published or forthcoming is breathtaking. On a comparative standard the contributors to the programme have clearly produced value for money. They have

> produced or (as is presently often the case)
> scheduled for publication in the coming year
> a very long list of books and other
> publications. On a quantitative scale this is a
> remarkable record, considering the relatively
> short programme period starting in 1994. To
> the knowledge of this reviewer, there have
> been other research programmes that didn't
> come up with a comparable list of
> publications after several years of research
> and after the spending of considerable
> amounts of money.

This is not, however, the strategic relevance of evaluation. The AHRB describes it as part of a dynamic, iterative process. 'Monitoring and evaluation is constructed as a loop,' explains Steve Morgan. 'It is not a linear process but feeds in policy at all levels, from the strategic level to the programme level.'

Accountability

Some may think a monitoring and evaluation process is how researchers are held to account for their work, but this is not the only function. Of course, at the programme level the board must see that public money is spent responsibly. At the next level, the monitoring and evaluation process also may pick up examples of both good and bad research practice. If these begin to combine into a common thread, then they can be seen and addressed. But the function is not solely to perform a watchdog role, as Steve further explained:

> This is not to force researchers to justify how
> and why they spent the money. I prefer to
> think of it in partnership terms. It can give us
> sufficient and significant information to allow
> us to explain what we do. It helps us in our
> representative role and allows us to be well-
> positioned to speak for the community to the
> wider society.

This happens by aggregating the information in various ways, by subject or scheme, for example. This allows the funder to assess not just the individual research outcome but also the wider impact, to conduct periodic reviews and respond to the 'so what?' factor. What, for example, has been the cumulative effect of all its funding in one particular subject area? If the Treasury asks the AHRB to justify how the study of poetry contributes to the socio-economic health of the nation, the AHRB will need to respond.

Another benefit of monitoring and evaluation is for the funder to assess itself internally. The process can reveal internal issues, perhaps of policy or structure, that may be thwarting the work of the funder or its award-holders. Steve Morgan's role, for example in 'Corporate Projects' is to help strategic decision-taking by conducting programme or scheme reviews.

Other funders will seek similar outcomes from evaluation. The ESRC says its evaluation serves three purposes: accountability (to make sure public money was spent properly), a project-based evaluation (to ensure the specific project was carried out properly, met its objectives and delivered both quality and impact) and feedback (to help researchers assess the project's quality and impact).

The value the researcher adds therefore extends beyond the immediate project and into the strategic objectives of the funder and the research community as a whole.

Presenting Value

Most awards ask the researcher for self-evaluation. This is to allow the award-holder to assess the experience, partly in terms of how the specific programme's aims and objectives were met, but also how it contributed to the wider academic community. It also reassures the funder that the research was conducted properly; if they are not satisfied, at the very least they may refuse final payment. In the worst case, the researcher's reputation will be seriously damaged.

Beyond just saying what the funder needs to hear as a bare requirement, the value of the experience needs articulating. If there is one thing successful researchers don't do at the evaluation stage, it is leave things to chance. This relates to issues discussed in the previous chapter about communication and keeping the relationship healthy. At this stage, there should be no surprises. Some researchers find themselves in the difficult position of having to explain retrospectively what should have been discussed throughout.

The experience of one researcher with some funders is less than complimentary:

> They hand over the money and in all honesty
> they don't really get any feedback at all until
> you do your final report two or three years
> from the point when it's been funded. Then,
> you do that in the form of a final report and at
> that stage, you've got to make the decision of
> saying do I tell them it was a project that
> didn't go according to plan and get a rating to
> reflect that, or do I tell them that it went
> according to plan and somehow dress it up,
> or alternatively tell them that it went
> according to plan and show what a good
> project it is. It really depends on the
> investigator and how much time and effort he
> can put into that process, but regardless,
> three years down the line is too long and
> you're at that stage where the money's been
> spent and you can't go back and correct
> anything. The very best case is that you learn
> from that process, that you can address some
> of the issues involved in managing projects if
> you get funded next time round.

Another researcher with experience in the corporate sector says that the final report is less of a problem if it is seen as just one in a series of communications:

> A lot of the ways in which the research pans
> out is actually a process of translation where
> you translate what they think they want to
> know into what you think they should think
> they should want to know. It's a negotiation
> involved.

That negotiation is only possible if the relationship has been strong and the researcher is regarded as someone who can act in partnership, while retaining academic credibility.

> I think it's important that that negotiation
> happens not from a sense of being terribly
> dependent but when we add a kind of bona
> fide, open, intellectual, academic quality to it.
> And that's important for us, and that's why it
> isn't a straightforward consultancy, and that's

> why it's different from a traditional
> consultancy. When one or other side tends to
> feel a dependency, that's when the quality of
> the research can be reduced or the integrity
> can go or you can find yourself asking
> questions which you don't feel particularly
> happy with.

Professor Mohamed Zairi, Director of the European Centre for Total Quality
Management at Bradford University, uses the concept of quality to evaluate
the benefit of his research projects. As we explored in earlier chapters, the
idea of what is good or of high quality is a relative concept, depending on who
is judging and for what purpose.

When he finishes a project, Mohamed asks himself whether, and how, it will
return a value to the funder and the wider community. Being published in a
journal, for example, is an important measure of recognition, but its value
may not be the same for everyone. Putting a more ethical spin on the
question, Mohamed says he asks himself what determines whether his work is
good:

> When you say I've done good work, people
> are forced to ask you the question: who has
> been the beneficiary? How did it affect them?
> What have been the benefits, what have been
> the outcomes? And you ought to be in a
> position to actually quantify tangible benefits.
> We ought to measure ourselves in the same
> way that the rest of the world does and we
> ought to include ourselves in that value chain
> principle.

Self-evaluation Checklist

Think through the evaluation carefully. The ESRC's end-of-award form[1]
asks the researcher to summarise the 'aims and objectives of the research,
noting briefly if these have changed since the original proposal'. Think
through this carefully in terms of what has been discussed above. By this
stage, any changes should have been communicated to the funder to forego
any surprises. The form also asks the researcher to explain, in less than 200
words:

---

1   www.esrc.ac.uk

suitable for a lay reader, the findings and
most significant achievements of the research.
The latter might include: theoretical
developments, new findings, new methods,
new datasets, impact of the research on
academics, policy-makers, practitioners etc.

Then, under a section called 'Dissemination, Nominated Outputs, Staffing,
Virements, Major Difficulties, Other Issues and Unexpected Outcomes,
Nominated Rapporteur' the ESRC asks for an executive summary of less
than 1 000 words describing the 'main research results in non-technical
language' plus a 5 000-word report describing research activities and results.

No matter what a particular funder's output formats may be, the challenge is
the same: how will you report on not just what you did but what it meant and
how it added value? As discussed in Chapter 4, your output reports should
incorporate the actual and expected out*comes*. This reminds us that not all the
criteria for success will be obvious or even shared. It will be up to the
researcher to make those connections and draw out the implications for
evaluation.

Ask yourself these questions to help form your response:

1   What was the original research question and was it answered?
2   Did the initial question change, and if so, why and how?
3   Did the research method follow the expected pattern?
4   How were any changes in the method anticipated, communicated and, if
    necessary, negotiated?
5   How did the research team interact, and what impact did that have on
    the project?
6   What specific outputs and outcomes were identified in the proposal, and
    were these delivered?
7   If changes to outputs occurred, why and how were these negotiated?
8   Was the research budget appropriate and what changes could have been
    made?
9   What were the thematic priorities and/or aims which the project was
    designed to address and how did this occur?
10 How did the project add value to the wider research programme (if
    appropriate)?
11 What research questions now present themselves?

Future Orientation

Finally, remember that evaluating research is important not just for securing final payment from a funder but also for opening up doors for future funding. You don't need a form or a checklist to know whether you have done good research; that isn't the only purpose of evaluation. At the very least, any researcher will evaluate their own research by asking 'What data do I have? What can I publish? What have I published?'

But, going further, one researcher described the next step:

> How and in what way has it allowed me to identify new research questions that can be put together in such a way that I can try and secure additional or new research funding? For me, that is the measure.

This may not correspond to the funder's measure, the same researcher notes. This may be framed more in terms of what the outputs were, and did it give them a solution to a problem or a further insight.

> I'm not saying I disagree with what they're looking at, it's an equally valid measure, but from my perspective, I'm interested in not just what can I publish or have I published it, but has it identified new questions for me to put together additional proposals for funding?

This future orientation points to a potential continuing relationship with the same funder, or a new relationship with a different funder. It is also what helps researchers become members of peer review panels or what prompts a funder to solicit their advice on proposed themes or programmes. Conducting a satisfactory evaluation that demonstrates both how you responsibly carried out research and how you enhanced the life of the academic community is what separates the great from the mundane. Most importantly, it will help position you not simply as a good researcher who can be trusted to do a good job, but as a colleague and important member within an academic community.

Conclusion

Funding bodies and funded researchers have a minimum level of evaluation required: were the specifications set out in the funding contract met? Did you, as a funded researcher, deliver what you said you would? This is, as we will explore in the following chapter, a minimum quality standard.

Funding bodies like the AHRB and ESRC need to be publically accountable for the research they are sponsoring. But that is not the sole aim of their monitoring and evaluation procedures. They see themselves as situated in the research community, contributing to improving the research process and research skills, and creating long-term societal benefits, as well as to make sure that a particular project has delivered on its promises.

To participate in this, you should, as a researcher, be looking to the future and considering outcomes of your research, but also, importantly, future research questions which can be explored. This may lead you into continuing relationships with your current funding body, or new ones with different funders.

Whatever the formal evaluation process demanded by the funding body, you should always rigorously self-evaluate your work. This is part of your own learning process, helping you do better research and to help others do good research in the future.

19 RESEARCH AND QUALITY MANAGEMENT

One of the most controversial concepts relating to academic institutions today is that of 'quality management'. It is a concept and practice important to researchers primarily because it is important to funders, be that indirect funders like government or direct funders like a corporate sponsor. It underpins much of the assessment processes within the academic sector in both teaching and research.

Unfortunately, much of what is meant and practised as 'quality management' in the non-academic world is misunderstood within the academic sector. This creates an antithesis and hostility which, at best, is destructive to researcher–funder relationships but, at worst, prevents people from applying the useful approaches of quality management. By using a reductionist approach, quality management will appear as a rigid framework focused on limitations and coercion. The reality, however, is much more nuanced and potentially of greater value for the researcher.

The 'Quality School'

God's specification to Moses for the construction of his temple (Exodus 25–28) resembles the most rigorous of ISO 9000-style quality assurance specifications. So long as people have organised endeavours – the building of the pyramids, Hannibal crossing the Alps, the construction of the great mediaeval cathedrals of Europe – quality management disciplines could be said to have been used. Codifying those principles is widely acknowledged to have originated with the works of Frederick Winslow Taylor in the early part of the twentieth century.

Taylor classified management as a science and, using principles of scientific method, sought out universal principles of management: the breaking of jobs into their simplest component parts, the arrangement of work flows in linear sequence, the selection and training of workers as specialists in performing these component tasks, and the incentivisation of workers to perform them as specified. US automotive pioneers Henry Ford (Ford Motor Company) and

Alfred Sloan (General Motors) famously adopted and executed Taylor's theories energetically.

But Taylor's principles (sometimes called 'Fordist' by social scientists, after Henry Ford) were challenged strongly by what arose as the human-relations school. Writers like Mary Parker Follett and the Harvard psychologist Elton Mayo in the USA, and Elliott Jacques in the UK, argued that to treat workers as units of production was dehumanising. Mayo cited strikes, sabotage and stock market collapse as the demonstrable failure of economic rationalism in business practice. The result is what now may be seen as a blend rather than an either/or in organisation addressed by a wider notion of quality management called Total Quality Management (TQM).

Total Quality Management

TQM proposes that a narrow view of manufacturing quality assurance was no longer effective when there were separate, expert, professional functions dealing with broad specialisations. TQM said that we should look at organisations as social organisms, like an ant colony, where a greater good should be put in place of individual (or departmental) self-interest.

One way of looking at TQM for research is to understand that it takes a systems perspective, not a piecemeal one. A good analogy is that of a clock. A systems perspective involves understanding how all the cogs work together to tell the time properly, and making sure that they do so together, rather than optimising the performance of individual units.

The humanistic interpretation of TQM says that people in organisations tend to behave in unpredictable ways, despite the creation of systematic structures. Therefore, the only way to achieve a 'total quality' orientation is by tapping into belief systems around some unifying values. By doing this, people will naturally use their intelligence and effort to gravitate towards a best outcome.

This view of TQM gave rise to the concept of the 'empowered' workforce – one in which internal controls are relaxed and lifted, and therefore power rests with each individual member, who is committed to 'do the right thing' given any particular circumstance.

The shapers of the modern TQM movement, most notably W. Edwards Deming, Joseph Juran and Philip Crosby, all combine a mixture of an engineering and a humanistic approach. Deming, in particular, argued that formal performance measurement systems produce bad quality, because people who feel others are judging them do not give of their best. Also, measurement systems more often than not measure the wrong things, which produces a sub-optimal result (back to the clock and the ant colony again).

Of the several schools of thought which exist in total quality management, there is one which should preoccupy us here for research purposes.

The rationale of that school runs thus: quality is not defined simply as 'fitness for purpose' or 'zero defects'. It is anything the 'customer' says it is. There is no absolute standard, but that does not mean there is no standard. Look at cars, for example. It is equally possible to drive to the office in a Ford economy model as it is in a Mercedes Benz. One is designed to meet a family's purposes for economy and size, while the other is designed to meet the wealthier, perhaps more status-conscious, person's need for conspicuous luxury. Both are 'quality' products.

People familiar with total quality management already know that the customer defines quality. The definition of whether something meets a customer's quality expectations is whether it is 'fit for the purpose' intended by the customer. The purpose, of course, is the customer's, not the producers.

How can we read this for the purpose of academe? Who is the 'customer' in the research process who defines quality and how do they define it? Whether the 'customer' is the person paying for the research to be conducted, or a peer reviewer deciding whether the work passes academic 'quality control', their ideas about quality should align with ours, the researchers.

It is therefore important to understand, within a quality management framework, that research can never deliver a standard product. How can it when, by definition, the question being explored will lead to an unknown answer? What the quality management framework allows, however, is that the customer – be that the funder, reviewer, assessor or student – can be assured that the process is reliable when the outcome is unknown.

Quality by Design

We have explored thus far how quality management came from two ideas about how to run organisations better. The first was, as introduced above, about customers. If we can learn what our customers like, and deliver it reliably, our customers will come back to us, tell others about us, and we will become more successful. Quality is therefore customer-driven: it depends on knowing customers' needs and fulfilling them reliably.

The second impetus behind the quality management movement was efficiency. If we can devise the most efficient way to produce a product or service we will be more successful. Quality is therefore about simplicity and 'designing out' potential mistakes from the beginning. Without managing quality, assuring and adding value become an impossible proposition. The earliest lessons of the quality movement, applicable to research funding, are those of:

- understanding what people want from research and delivering it to match those needs ('fitness for purpose'). This means looking carefully at the organisation and discovering their strategic aims. What is their driving ethos or the particular programme's link to their wider aims?
- drawing detailed specifications based on the articulated customer needs, and delivering carefully to them in a proposal ('conformance to specification'). This is how researchers write a proposal to demonstrate that they understand the objectives of the organisation and specific programme;
- identifying and managing the variables in the research process which can lead to deviation from specification ('process control'). Although research is likely to evolve, it cannot be allowed to drift off the original proposal without renegotiating or at least informing the funder about the changes and implications;
- keeping detailed records of the process, allowing deviations to be traced and rectified to promote transparency and evaluation ('quality audit/document control'). This is increasingly important for evaluation purposes and the needs for funding organisations to be transparent and publicly accountable.

Quality and Diversity

A pervasive misconception about quality management is that it stresses uniformity and conformity. Quality is more than replication or rigidity. What about the quality of, say, a novel by a favourite author, or a song by a favourite band? They cannot be the same as the last one we read or listened to, or we wouldn't bother to read them or buy their recordings. For some goods and services, and for research in particular, the question of 'the same' has to be thought about a bit more carefully. Particularly in the academic sector, people are prone to confuse reliability with replication. Good research processes, for example, may be reliably designed to produce interesting or surprising conclusions – reliably.

In other words, although quality assurance is essentially about following appropriate processes as effectively as possible, the principle which drives effective quality assurance is continual questioning. Behind quality assurance are dynamic questions, which are always looking to provoke change. Nothing stands still.

Customer expectations do not stand still either. This will be obvious as the relationship develops, if the researcher is open to the notion of changing needs. For a researcher wanting to work with a funder more than once, it would be sensible to stay attuned to their changing views of quality. We discussed earlier the idea of a customer-driven definition of quality which says that 'quality is in the eye of the beholder' or 'quality is what the customer says it is'. Sometimes a customer-driven definition of quality is expressed as 'delighting' a customer or of exceeding expectations.

Some researchers, for example, will wait until the deadline or even beyond it before submitting a report, just because they know they can get away with it. Looking from a customer perspective, that may not be their expectation or what gives them a positive feeling about working with the researcher in the future. But, problematically, when expectations are regularly exceeded, a new expectation benchmark is set. If you expect a report on time and you start getting it a few days early, you might be 'delighted' but after the tenth time, you are not delighted any more. You have come expect it. Your standards have become higher. If you expect the phone to be answered by the fifth ring and it's answered on the second, you may be delighted. If it happens a few more times you'll begin to expect it. You may even hang up on the fourth ring.

This poses a knotty problem; it is the difference between 'creating quality', through meeting and sometimes exceeding expectations, and 'avoiding non-quality', which is done by avoiding a slip below expectations. This point is an important one, for it marks a crucial difference in philosophies of quality management. It is as if quality is a scale with zero in the middle, positive numbers on one side and negatives on the other:

Lower than expected	Expected quality levels	Higher than expected
−3 −2 −1	0	+1 +2 +3

Meeting expectations, which from the organisation's point of view, represents 'quality', only gets to zero in the customer's eyes. No value is added. Another way to think of it is using the example of air travel. We expect to arrive at our destination in one piece, with our bags coming off the carousel. However, if that happens, we do not say, 'Wow, that was a high quality flight! We didn't crash, and our bags got here!' It's what we expect.

Creating quality in airline services means getting above the zero point of expectations. Airlines tackle that issue through innovations in ticketing, check-in, food and beverage services, humour (some airlines have a policy where the attendants make jokes and have games and competitions in-flight), movies, seat-back TV, in-flight phone services and so on. But if a wing falls off in flight, no innovations in food or movies will make up for that. It will become, by definition, a low quality experience.

Imagine if you saw a researcher's advertisement: 'Academic service. No spelling mistakes and references double-checked professionally.' Wouldn't that cause you to pause for a moment? Why would an academic researcher say such things: isn't accuracy a basic requirement and a necessary condition? These may be described as 'static' components which meet customer baseline expectations: accurate typing, appropriate methodology, professional creativity. What are the dynamic components which can grow and change as the customer relationship grows? For, as we explored in this book, the primary focus is on relationships. As each customer is unique, so is each relationship. Never neglect the static components. They are the ones which get you to the zero-base of meeting expected quality levels. The dynamic components will, from that base, *create* quality.

Understanding the nature of those relationships will help us determine the meaning of quality for our different customers. We need to find ways to add value, but also to maintain consistent quality in the most fluid and flexible way possible. Researchers need to continually ask:

1 How well do you understand your funding partner's expectations, and how do you monitor them for change?
2 How do you define quality research? Does this exceed the customer's expectations?
3 How do you differentiate consistently, created adding value that the customer says is important?

Conclusion

There are few – or no – absolutes in managing quality. The simplest and most robust principle is that management for quality assures fitness for purpose. Which of course gives rise to the questions: Whose purpose? What purpose? How do we know when it is 'fit'?

One of the great advances of the quality revolution of, particularly, the later twentieth century, was the elimination of unpleasant surprises for customers and consumers. If you pay for a litre, you get a litre. If you eat something certified as edible, it won't poison you. If you buy a new car, the wheels won't fall off. Or, at least, not very often.

But fitness for purpose, as defined as something which will satisfy or delight a customer or consumer, does not in all cases mean a standard product. It does mean a *reliable* product. Research by its nature can never deliver a standard product. How can it when, by definition, the question being explored will lead to an unknown answer? But applying quality assurance principles to research means that customers and consumers can be assured that the process is reliable, even when the outcome is unknown.

The guiding disciplines of quality management in businesses and other organisations fit very happily with the research process. It is important for researchers to make their research *fit for purpose*, which involves a full understanding of what the purpose is, and whose purpose it is. From this investigation of purpose comes a specification for the research, which leads to the second great rule of managing quality – *conformance to specification* – making a promise and delivering on it. To be able to do so reliably necessitates understanding what the variables are which can mess up delivery of a research process which reliably satisfies customers and consumers. These variables within the process must be subjected to *process control*, so you can manage them. And finally, the fourth great rule of managing quality, again absolutely applicable to scholarly research, is to make sure your records about the research are clear and honest. This *document control* allows you to learn from the process, to intervene to address problems, and to leave a good audit trail for evaluation.

Just doing what is expected is necessary, but it's not normally seen as quality. It's normally seen as what is expected. To create the experience of quality for your funding partner, try to find ways to go a little way beyond expectations. Then you may find that if you deliver on your promises, and exceed the expectations of your partner, you will gain yourself a reputation as someone who is a pleasure to work with, who can deliver high quality work.

And that's not a bad thing to aspire to.

20 WRITING BETTER, WRITING FASTER

The final two chapters explore the importance of understanding the needs of those involved in the publishing process and how to target and focus on the right publication. But first, this chapter looks at how to hasten the writing process while maintaining quality and integrity.

The First Draft: Structure

The twentieth century American writer Thomas Wolfe once remarked on the difficulty of being a writer:

> What I had to face, the very bitter lesson that
> everyone who wants to write has got to learn,
> was that a thing may in itself be the finest
> piece of writing one has ever done, and yet
> have absolutely no place in the manuscript
> one hopes to publish.

His observation can remind us that writing is about communication, not just reflection. That means it must be contextual. For the purpose of research funding, it means communicating with specific audiences for specific purposes.

Clear thinking leads to clear writing. Just as we saw in Chapter 13, a well-written piece of work reflects an underlying clarity and purpose. What some people call 'writer's block' is usually nothing more than unclear thinking. Consider the piece carefully before rushing into writing it.

Think of a paper as a dialogue with the reader, structuring the paper to answer your reader's questions as they arise. Any paper should have a beginning, middle, and an end, evident to the reader. En route through the paper, the reader needs to know not only what is being said at the time, but also where it is leading. Some may argue that a more individualistic and idiosyncratic style is preferable, but the truth is, any communication's objective is to achieve understanding with the reader, and unless one is a very skilled writer indeed, this is best achieved by following some clear signposted steps. The more idiosyncratic we become, the more barriers we may raise. People who become too self-conscious of their personal style begin to lose respect for the reader's needs.

A sensible structure will have a strong beginning to explain to the reader:

- the purpose of your paper
- why it is important
- to whom it is important
- what they will discover by reading it.

Once the reader is oriented to those questions, another obvious one arises: who are you? What they need now is background. Explain who you are and why you tackled the problem. Remind them of the reasons everyone in the field has been searching for such answers.

This should be an easy section to write. You are aware of the problem and what other people have said about it. The purpose of this section is to provide context, lend credibility to what you say and reassure the reader.

Now the readers are genuinely interested, but they have moved into a more critical phase. They are asking questions such as how did you decide to go about it? This is resonant, again, of funders who have described their frustration with authors who do not describe their method.

In a classic research student's textbook, *The Management of a Student Research Project* (Sharp, Peters and Howard 2002, 3rd edition), the authors gave the following advice to authors of research papers, based on the reader's thought process:

> Question–answer: Every time you generate a question – 'But, what is the critical variable?' – the reader will expect an answer to follow quickly.

> Problem–solution: When you describe a problem, the reader wants to know what the solution is or, if there is not one, why not.

> Cause–effect/effect–cause: Cause and effect – if this, then that – must be linked, in whatever order you present it.

General–specific: When making a general or sweeping statement the reader will want to see how you qualify it with specific examples and evidence. The converse is also true. When you make specific statements the reader will want to know if that comment can be generalised. Adding to the body of knowledge usually requires generalisation, but not to the point of obscurity.

Having explained the method, your reader is now asking 'So what?' How did your approach work in practice? This section is not simply descriptive but also analytical. What happened and why? This is a critical phase of your work. This is where you show your ability to reflect on your methodology and offer constructive comments about how you, or others, might approach it differently next time.

Next, you need to offer your findings and analysis. Remember to relate this to your research question. By now you will have noted the critical implications of your work and analysed them from the reader's perspective. You prepared the reader to expect certain reassurances, and now is the time to give them. Prove yourself here.

Finally, your readers are wondering what it all means. This is where you make your conclusions, again tied back to the research question, and articulate implications. Relate the implications to your previous sections by summarising the key points of your argument and your findings.

Consider the reader as someone whose interest in your work may only be peripheral, or who may be a student approaching the subject for the first time. You need to help the reader identify and articulate the worth of your work.

That is why stating implications is not something to be left as an afterthought in the last paragraph. Implications must direct the paper from the beginning and inform the structure. Knowing your implications helps you decide what to include in your paper and what to leave out.

Ask yourself essential questions:

- What wider principles emerged from your research?
- How can people in your field use it?
- Can people in other fields use it?

- How can other researchers take your work forward?
- How can your research be applied in practice?
- Who is able to apply your findings?
- What might they do?
- When and where might it be done?
- How might they approach it?

The answers to some of these questions may be 'don't know' or 'not applicable'. Which ones do apply, and what are your answers?

If your paper has implications for further research, look at the implications of your method. Each decision needs to be explained. For example:

- What were the implications of your scope and limitations?
- What were the implications of choosing particular methods of data gathering and analysis?
- Did certain techniques cast some doubts or further veracity on your findings?
- What did the literature say and how does it matter to your research?
- How did your methodology affect the findings?
- What are the implications of other potential answers to the problem?
- How far are you prepared to go and why?

Do not leave it to your reader to guess. Don't wait for a reviewer to say that a 'surprising result' would not have been particularly surprising if the authors had thought at the beginning of the study what they might expect to find.

Now that you have mapped out your paper, it is a good idea to return to the introduction to make sure that you have included the main points. Reviewing your introduction ensures that you will not inadvertently miss a point which may only have occurred to you strongly in the body of your paper.

The Finishing Touch

It is a good start to have a first draft outline paper prepared which reflects your focus. Many people lose confidence at the next stage because they worry that they do not write well. It is important to remember now that people normally can write well when they think clearly, and that even experienced and skilled writers do not write well when they do not think clearly. You should be in a position now to relax and apply the finishing touch to your work.

Engage with the Reader

In the discussion in Chapter 6 on what is meant by 'good' research, one of the points which many researchers emphasised strongly was the notion of accessibility and engagement, that good research is accessible to all sorts of people and engages people. The involvement of the person, perhaps even a non-scholar, reading the research is part of what makes it good.

So how can you make sure your work engages people? Firstly, you have to understand the people with whom you are communicating, but if you reviewed carefully the points in the previous chapter, you will have done that. Next, you have to make sure you are using language and tone that ease understanding. There are three main pitfalls to avoid.

VERBOSITY

Why take 200 words to say something when 50 will do? If you originally thought the section was only going to need 200 words, why are you still writing after 750? It is probably because you have become carried away by your own thoughts and lost touch with what the reader needs. You may have become unsure of what you are trying to say, so you keep circling around, avoiding coming to a conclusion.

To keep the focus, return to our first draft outline plan. Remember what you had already worked out. Discipline yourself to write less than you want and remember that reviewers are unimpressed by long, turgid sentences.

JARGON

Jargon is a private shorthand that sometimes helps us communicate quickly to those who know the same jargon. We may be familiar with it, our colleagues may be familiar with it, but the reader may be lost.

Read your material carefully and ask yourself whether your readers will understand. If you have any doubt, change the word or phrase into user-friendly language. Examine the concepts that you have borrowed. Best of all, have someone outside your field read it. Is it likely that people unfamiliar with your work will understand? Most journals, however specialised, are unwilling to accept articles only decipherable by a small group of specialists. Be especially careful of acronyms.

IMPRESSIVE WORDS

Use words to express, not to impress. The best writing is always the simplest and the clearest. Is there really a good reason to use that longer or more complex word? The best way to avoid using the wrong word is to keep your words as simple as possible. Use your dictionary, but throw away your thesaurus. Too often, people consult a thesaurus to find a bigger, more important-sounding word for the more common, more familiar word. If you are going to use a thesaurus, use it the other way round, to move from the complex to the simple.

Testing your Paper

Finally, put your work to the test. Ask a colleague or friend to help you. It does not matter if they are familiar with your subject area; indeed, it may be preferable that they are not. Ask them to assess your paper by browsing it quickly, using five criteria:

- **Purpose:** clearly stated on the first page?
- **Key points:** logically flowing from point to point with signposting, such as subheadings, introductions and conclusions to sections?
- **Implications:** clearly specified, with special attention to who the implications are for and what readers can do next?
- **Readability:** jargon-free, familiar words, reasonably short sentences, easy to follow theme?
- **Appeal:** would they go back and read the paper more thoroughly?

This exercise models what we readers – you, they and I – do all the time. We scan, we browse, we sift. Readers want access to the right information they can understand and use. Given a choice between a turgid, vague, obscure paper and a paper which reveals what you are looking for, which one would you choose?

Once you think you are happy with your paper, think again. Do not be your own proof-reader. Our brains allow us to compensate for our own errors. We know what we meant to say and our eye can trick us into seeing what we intended, but not necessarily what is there.

Have more than one other person read it carefully. Take their advice. If something you have said is not clear to your reader, do not bother explaining it face-to-face. It simply has not worked. Rewrite it.

The next and final chapter deals with being published. Being published means you have joined and been recognised by a wider community of published authors, editors, and reviewers. As funders make it more apparent that dissemination is a priority, you can increase your skills correspondingly. That will mean that you can write papers more quickly without losing any quality. Funders, above all, understand the constraints of time. As the AHRB says in its guidance notes for the Research Leave scheme:[1]

> One of the most precious research commodities is time. The AHRB's Research Leave Scheme relieves individual scholars from teaching and administrative duties, providing the time needed to conclude a research project.

Writing for publication not only satisfies the requirements of your funders. It helps position yourself in your career. To position yourself further, consider becoming more active in the publishing process. Many well-known, internationally-respected editors began with just one section of a journal to look after – the research news, for example, or forthcoming events. You may become a reviewer, looking at papers in your field and offering constructive advice to other authors. Communicating your work to others and assisting other people to do the same is intensely satisfying.

Perhaps more importantly, returning to the beginning thoughts of this book, you have something important to contribute. The more practised you become at writing and dissemination of your research, the more people will be informed, influenced and excited by your work.

Conclusion

Writing with clarity means writing with purpose. Many people who experience 'writer's block' are in fact experiencing a lack of clarity, which may lead to a lack of confidence about writing skills.

This chapter has explored different aspects of clarity, starting with the premise that we are conducting a silent dialogue with the reader. Your structure therefore reflects the thinking processes of the reader, anticipating questions and systematically providing relevant information. Most importantly, we have stressed here the need to remain focused on both your research questions and implications, answering the prime 'so what?' question.

1   www.ahrb.ac.uk/research/index.htm

Techniques which correspond to clear writing include brevity, avoiding jargon, keeping language clear and simple, and always remembering your reader. This will enliven your writing as you engage with your reader and seek to express, rather than impress.

Finally, authors are encouraged to share their work. Having someone else look at it provides an opportunity for feedback and revision. Remember that the more often you review your own work, the more it becomes 'normalised' in your own mind. An outsider can spot mistakes and vagueness which you, with your familiarity with the paper, may easily miss.

21 PUBLICATION PLANNING

The issue of dissemination has appeared and reappeared throughout this work. The pressure to publish is felt by salaried academics who must submit published works for the Research Assessment Exercise. The main problem is time, or rather the lack of it. Many cite additional administrative requirements imposed by, for example, quality management systems. Other limitations are imposed by financial considerations which often restrict the number of faculty. This creates additional workloads for existing faculty who must juggle teaching, administrative duties, researching and writing.

Contract researchers also have severe time constraints. How are contract researchers expected to find the time to write, particularly when nobody is paying them for that time?

'You have to have a programme to do it,' says Jane Hunt, an experienced contract researcher working with the Centre for the Study of Environmental Change at Lancaster University. As she explains, the pattern of contract research means that the next proposal is always being written as the next source of funding is being sought.

This chapter is about developing, in Jane's words, 'the programme to do it' by making the best use of the limited time available. The programme begins with focusing on your specific purpose, which will help you develop the right publishing strategy.

Why Publish?

Just as you did when putting together a research proposal, you must now review your reasons for making this effort. Why do you want to be published? Different people will have different reasons and priorities.

TO BECOME KNOWN

Some funders proactively search for researchers using published works as a major source of enquiry. Becoming published is therefore important not just to please other academics but to make yourself known to future funders. Being published increases the chances of being invited to conferences, being asked to review papers and join advisory boards. It opens and strengthens networks and helps you promote your work, your skills, and your interests.

TO GET RICH

You will not be paid for a journal article and any book royalties you receive will be paltry. Becoming known through publications may, however, be a key to future funding.

TO GET A BETTER JOB

Being published and recognised in a particular field helps enormously with academic careers, particularly as they relate to research assessment funding. People who can communicate well with their peers are in demand. Research itself is worthless unless it is disseminated. For academics and many professionals, this usually happens with publication. Too often, fine work is not recognised simply because no one knows about it. That means that future work is compromised and the possibilities of working near the top of the field become limited.

BECAUSE THE RESEARCH MATTERS

This is one of the strongest reasons. Believing in your research and its value will be a motivating factor. The danger here is not targeting the right audience and concluding, wrongly, that the research is worthless because it is not published.

BECAUSE YOU HAVE TO

This is how some people explain the propensity to publish. It is not a choice, for them, but a demand. In one sense, of course, there is an obligation which comes with the vocation and often with the funding. You belong to a body of knowledge which only grows as people add to it. Writing up your findings or articulating your concepts is your way of contributing to the academic community, potentially for generations to come.

TO LEARN THROUGH OTHERS

A published paper or book represents only part of a lifelong membership in a community. It is through beginning and maintaining contact with that community that we are able to receive the comments and the responses that will tell us more about our field and ourselves. Sometimes feedback can lead to collaboration from unexpected sources.

Feedback and collaboration are valuable components of the publishing process – and they are free. Referees and reviewers will decide if your work will be accepted, rejected or sent back for revision. 'Revise' feedback usually includes precise comments about which parts of the paper should be revised, and often how; even papers which are rejected are often rejected for a well-articulated reason. Some people might call it rejection. Let's call it learning.

TO GAIN CLARITY

Nobody, not even a professional writer, can write without focus. What people call writer's block is usually nothing more than lack of focus. What are you trying to say? Unless you know the answer to that, the words will not come easily.

As we write, we structure our thinking and put sometimes difficult and abstract concepts into words. We ask ourselves if it makes sense – even better, we ask others if it makes sense to them. We write, we edit, we revise, and we do everything we can to make our argument and our evidence clear.

The Programme to Do it

Once you have articulated your reasons for publishing, the next step is to create a publishing plan. Given that time is scarce, we do not want it squandered on activities which will fail.

The ideal time to create the plan is at the beginning of your research. In its guidance notes, the ESRC makes the point that researchers must involve the people who will be affected by the research outcomes:

> The Council's new mission places emphasis on ensuring that researchers engage as fully as possible with the users of research outcomes. These may be other academics, government departments, public bodies, businesses, voluntary organisations or other interested parties. Try to consult with and involve people who could make a valuable contribution to the research and who could provide support and interest. Try to do this in

the planning of the project and build
dissemination activities into the structure of
your research plan rather than give them
passing reference as an afterthought at the
end.

Here, we will explore the single most important success criterion in academic publishing: targeting the right publication. Just like unsuccessful research proposals, many unsuccessful journal articles and book proposals have simply been sent to the wrong place. On average, half of all journal papers are rejected before they enter the review process, simply because they have been sent to the wrong journal. Busy people who do not have time to waste need to spend more time on choosing the right publication.

How can you improve your targeting skills? Most of us do not appreciate the many ways a single piece of research can be directed to different audiences. Borrowing a model from the world of business, the strategic writer Igor Ansoff (Ansoff, 1965) provided organisations with a model to help them plan what to do with their products and potential markets. He suggested that there are four variables that offer different opportunities when differently combined: new products, existing products, new markets, existing markets. Translating this concept to papers and journals we might look at it this way:

UNDEVELOPED PAPERS TO UNFAMILIAR JOURNALS

This is the riskiest option. We have not yet tested our ideas by writing them down and we know nothing about the journal we are targeting. Unfortunately, that is where many new writers start – and stop.

UNDEVELOPED PAPERS TO FAMILIAR JOURNALS

This is an improvement on the previous option. The paper may be yet undeveloped, but at least we are familiar with the journal. This can guide us towards structuring and writing the paper.

DEVELOPED PAPERS TO UNFAMILIAR JOURNALS

You have written a paper, and it may be brilliant, but you are now increasing your risk of rejection by sending it to an unfamiliar journal. You will have to work hard to become familiar with the journal before you finalise your paper.

In principle, it is a good idea to widen the field as much as possible. Too many authors restrict themselves to the one or two journals they know, without finding out about related journals. Sending a paper to a high-demand journal with a rejection rate of 98 per cent is a rather discouraging way to start. It may be better to practise on a journal that has several hundred, rather than several thousand, papers from which to choose.

DEVELOPED PAPERS TO FAMILIAR JOURNALS

Creative authors can derive several papers from a single piece of research in this way. Some journals will accept nothing less than being the first to report the findings, while others will want particular sections emphasised. For example, your main paper may be an 8 000-word detailed description of the research just completed and the key findings. Your objective may be to report the findings for the first time and you have therefore selected a journal positioned as a publication of original, new research findings. Having published in that journal, you may look again at the paper and decide to reduce it in total but expand the methodology section for a journal specialising in method.

Finding the Right Publication

Most editors say that many of the manuscripts or book proposals they receive do not even reach the review stage. They are immediately rejected because they do not meet the editorial objectives of the publisher. This is exactly what we have seen happens with many research proposals.

Why would that be so? Undoubtedly, it is because the author did not research the problem. Perhaps the author did not bother to investigate the publisher's objectives, or perhaps the paper or proposal was rejected by the author's initial preferred journal and simply sent on to the next without revision. Or maybe the author just did not know how to research the targeted journal.

Let's start from there, from a position of relative ignorance, and just as we did when looking at proposals, understand that the hard work is the first, exploratory stage. The objective must be to find the right publisher suitably matched to your work. There are several ways to do this.

NETWORKS WITHIN YOUR RESEARCH COMMUNITY

You probably know who is respected in your field and who is writing about topics closely linked to yours. You can find out where these authors are published by carrying out a search by author in your library. You can also find out where those who cite them are being published by referring to a citation index.

Ask your colleagues which routes of dissemination they recommend. Find out which journals or book publishers matter most to those in a position to judge you. Which are rated most highly by your colleagues? Which do funders cite, both public and private? The unavoidable rule about being judged by other people is to always find out what criteria they are using. If your reference group rates one journal or book publisher more highly than another, you need to know – and why.

Ask fellow researchers. What do the people you most respect read? What do they have to say about the journals or publishers you have shortlisted? Where do they publish, and where did they publish first? What alternatives do they know to those you have selected?

Understanding your Chosen Publication and Editorial Team

The first level of assessment just described will give you a brief overview of the dissemination possibilities that might be suitable. From there, you can find the names and addresses of journals and publishers. Unfortunately, this first step is the one which seems to complete the process for many would-be authors. As most researchers will publish in journals as the key method of dissemination, this section describes ways to become more familiar with a journal. Before you write your paper, you will need a thorough idea of the journal's requirements. Finding these out is easy but takes time.

READING POTENTIAL PUBLICATIONS

The best way to become familiar with a journal is to read it. Copies may be available in your own library, in hard copy or via an online collection, or the librarian may be able to obtain them through interlibrary loans. But, remembering the pressures of time, you will not be able to read every issue. Be selective. The first and last issues in any one volume (year) are those which will probably contain the most clues since it is in these issues that strategically-minded editors discuss their objectives. In the first issue, editors will often describe what themes are to come. As they anticipate the new year, they will also often comment on the kinds of papers they hope to receive, or the improvements they will be making to the journal. In the final issue, editors will often summarise the year's contributions and comment on what they consider to be the high and low points.

Book publishers often publish series of books which have editorials introducing key themes and publishing objectives. It is worthwhile reading single volumes as well, to absorb the publisher's particular emphasis and style.

NOTES TO AUTHORS

All journals publish guidance notes for prospective authors which include the editorial objectives and notes on house style. These may not appear in each issue but there will at least be a reference to them and to the issue in which they appear.

Book publishers also provide guidance notes for authors articulating their requirements and outlining how to write a proposal.

MEETING THE NEEDS OF THE EDITORIAL TEAM

Beyond the technical points just described, it is important to understand the people involved. As with most publishing, scholarly journal publishing relies on several layers of people to help your work reach the final reader in the best shape possible. Each person has compatible, but slightly different, needs and pressures. Each will approach the paper and individual journal with slightly different questions.

> *Author:* Can I get my paper accepted in this journal?
> *Editor:* Does it meet the aims of the journal and its audience?
> *Review board:* Is it the right quality?
> *Reader:* Where can I read it? Is it useful to me?

Each person or group involved has a need to fulfil. If they understand the others' needs, they are more likely to be able to satisfy them. As an author, you might find you can publish regularly in the same journal or even another journal published by the same distributor. This brings you to the ultimate goal: how to repeat the performance, and possibly, if desired, move towards assuming reviewing and editing roles yourself.

It will help to get to know your partners in the publishing process a little better.

UNDERSTANDING EDITORS

Editors are respected within their institutions and their academic community and are, by definition, busy people. They are normally extremely active, time-pressured people constantly involved in teaching, researching, writing and editing.

Editing a journal will, during an average year, involve hundreds of extra hours of work. The editor's job extends beyond receiving papers. It includes: advising the publisher on the direction of the journal; agreeing editorial strategy; appointing a review board; monitoring the workings of the review board to ensure quality and timeliness; accepting articles for the review process; corresponding with reviewers; taking their feedback and passing it on to the author; seeing the paper through one or several revisions; making sure all the documentation is in order; selecting which issue the paper should appear in based on pagination requirements and editorial balance; sending it to the publisher in time for the agreed production schedule; looking over the proofs; answering queries from sub-editors; and finally sending the approved version back to the publisher on schedule.

Editors agree that a main reason they take on the extra work is to keep ahead in the field and to keep in touch. Many say that one of the most exciting parts of their job is to promote the careers of new scholars as well as seeking good work from established scholars. For an editor, some authors are good news, and some not so good. Some make their lives easier and some make them difficult.

What can you do to smooth the publication process?

- Meet the aims of the journal.
- Conform to specifications given in the Notes for Authors.
- Respond promptly with requests for revision, corrections and so on.
- Keep to deadlines.
- Complete all documentation fully and promptly.
- Carefully check your paper so it is word-perfect on submission. Don't amend proofs, other than printer's errors.

Doing all the above can ease an acceptable paper through the process and help build a positive relationship with the editor.

UNDERSTANDING REVIEWERS

Reviewers are expected to remain anonymous, but in any field their number is limited. Who are these mysterious arbiters of quality? They are people like you, often people you know, professors at your own university, someone who presented a paper at a recent conference. The benefits they derive from their work are similar to the benefits experienced by editors. They keep up to date in their own fields, they keep in touch with who is writing interesting papers based on original thought or research, and they improve their own reputation by being associated with a good-quality journal. Reviewers might read anything from one or two papers a year to several papers each month. They read each carefully and in detail so that they can send constructive comments back.

The review process is normally a 'blind' one, meaning the editor knows who the author is and to which reviewers he or she is sending the paper, but authors don't know who is reviewing it and reviewers don't know who the author is because the editor has removed the author's name and affiliation from the front of the paper. Editors will normally send a reviewer papers that reflect that individual's own subject knowledge, expertise and interest. The author can therefore assume that the paper is being read by someone who is not only a recognised leader in the field, but someone who reads papers similar to the author's regularly and thoroughly.

The conclusions they reach and advice they give are serious, considered, and free.

UNDERSTANDING READERS

Reviewers and editors often note that an author did not view the paper 'through the reader's eyes'. The reader may be a student, approaching the subject for the first time, or a renowned expert. As an author, you need to know what benefits they seek. What you can expect is that, being fellow members of your knowledge community, they too are busy. How will you help them gain the requisite knowledge from your paper as easily as possible?

Often, the reader's main question is 'so what?' They do not want to know that you did research, but how and why and what the findings and implications were. This means you must be clear about structuring and writing your paper to help meet those needs. It is hard to review your own work to see if you have been as clear as possible.

Managing the Review Process

By now, you know which journal you are targeting, you have written and proof-checked a publishable paper, you have followed the journal's house style notes and will now submit it according to their requirements. Always enclose a covering letter stating your name, the title of the paper, brief paragraph describing the contents and stating why you chose the specific journal (this applies to an email submission as well as a hard copy one). If there has been previous correspondence relating to a synopsis or a telephone call, refer to it and to any further guidance from the editor which was given at that time.

Your manuscript, even if it is addressed to the editor, will normally be received first by a secretary or editorial assistant. The details from your covering letter will sometimes be logged into a diary system for future correspondence. You should receive an acknowledgement saying that your paper has been received. That does not mean that it has been sent into the review stream, remembering that usually half of all papers are rejected before that stage.

The papers that do survive that initial assessment will enter the review system. For a fully refereed journal the process is, as discussed earlier, at least double-blind. This may take several weeks or months. If you have not heard back within 12 weeks, it would be reasonable to contact the journal and ask about its progress. In many cases it may simply be sitting on someone's desk awaiting attention.

The reviewers' comments are returned to the editor with one of three recommendations. One, rarely, is to accept the paper as it is. Very few papers are perfect. The second is to ask the author to revise the paper in view of the reviewer's comments. The third is to reject it outright.

Being asked to revise an article is a compliment. Ask experienced authors what it is they value most in the publishing process and the answer will most often be one word: feedback. It means that you are regarded as a potential contributor to the journal and therefore also as a potential contributor to the body of knowledge. Do not be disappointed with being asked to revise; it means the reviewers and editors feel you are worth the effort. They are willing to invest time in you. You should view this process not as extra work but as extra, free, support and advice.

Sometimes, less experienced authors create unnecessary trouble for an editor. Once an article is marked 'revise' it will be sent back to you with an invitation to revise it within a certain period. Respond to the editor immediately, agreeing to make the suggested revisions by the date given. Then, without fail, stick to it. Missing deadlines because you are 'too busy' is an insult to busy editors and reviewers.

Once you send your paper back to the editor, it will be reviewed again. Sometimes, your revisions will adequately reflect their expectations and sometimes they will ask you to go even further. The same principles as we discussed above apply: do your best to respond to their requests, and tell them you are doing so.

If your paper is rejected it may mean that it is a brilliant paper but not brilliant enough to compete with the 30 other brilliant papers the editor has received. You should then consider why. A rejected paper means that the editor and reviewers do not feel it could be appropriate for the readership even if amendments were made. Why would they think that?

- Your paper did not meet the editorial objectives of the journal (poor targeting).
- Your paper was poorly written, badly structured, badly argued.
- Your paper was good, but just not as good as some of the others.

We must assume now that, if you have done your research properly, targeted the journal correctly, structured your article, written it well and followed the journal's Notes for Authors, only the latter could possibly apply. In this case, look for another journal in the same field and revise accordingly.

Once the editorial team has accepted your manuscript, it will enter the production process. This is where the work is reformatted into the journal's house style, with the figures, tables and illustrations brought into the correct format and the whole paper checked for any errors which were not caught by the author or reviewers

The author will then receive proofs to check for errors which went unnoticed by the production team or to double-check changes that may have been made by the sub-editors. It is not, however, expected that the author will disagree with changes made for reasons of house style. There are several accepted spellings of certain words and phrases that will ultimately be decided by the journal's editorial team.

Looking over proofs is very difficult for many authors. Each time we see our work we will be tempted to change it. We can always write a little more clearly; there is always a sentence that can be improved; there is always something more we can say. Unfortunately, making changes at proof stage only slows the process. The changes will have to be incorporated and double-checked. Some publishers charge authors who do this, reflecting the additional cost and burden it causes. But, remember: there are perfect papers, and there are published papers. Authors must discipline themselves to let their work go.

Conclusion

Publication is an important part of funded research, both for the funder and for the researchers. But publications don't just flow naturally out of a research project. They need work, and they need a plan.

The most important piece of research in publication planning is finding the right journal to match your research project. If you are familiar with one or more journals, having published there before, you may have a good feeling for how likely you are to get a paper derived from the research project accepted.

If not, it is important, to save time and rejections or heavy revisions, to find out which will be the best publication(s) to fit your work. Colleagues, research administrators and directors may be able to advise on which journals will carry the most weight in their field, if you are unsure. Make sure you read the notes for authors on any target journal, and consider engaging with the editor by sending an abstract or summary of your prospective paper. If it is deemed not to fit for whatever reason, you have saved a lot of time, and can move on to another prospective outlet.

Being published, whether as a journal paper, a book or even a piece in a trade magazine or newspaper, may be a specified, or at least a highly desirable outcome. In any case, it is invariably a very worthwhile task for most researchers, in terms of personal career advancement and profile.

But being published needs a disciplined programme. Write a clear plan, with timings, and share it with colleagues and, if appropriate, your funding agency. It will demonstrate that you are concerned with outputs beyond the report itself.

BIBLIOGRAPHY

Ansoff, H.I. (1965), *Corporate Strategy*, New York: McGraw-Hill.

Day, Abby (1996), *How to Get Research Published in Journals*, Aldershot: Gower.

Jung, Carl Gustav (1938), *Psychological types or the psychology of individuation*, London: Kegan Paul.

Martin, Emily (1994), *Flexible Bodies*, Boston: Beacon Press.

Skeggs, Beverley (1997), *Formations of Class and Gender*, London: Sage.

Orwell, George (1957), 'Politics and the English Language', *Inside the Whale and Other Essays*, London: Penguin.

Sharp, John A., Peters, J. and Howard, K. (2002), *The Management of a Student Research Project*, 3rd edition, Aldershot: Gower.

INDEX

How to Get Research Published in Journals

Abby Day

You've finished the research, and you realize it's worth publishing.
Your colleagues think so too. You know publication will enhance both
your own standing and that of your organization. So what's stopping you?
Lack of time? An unconscious fear of rejection? Conflicting priorities?
In this, the first book to address the subject, Abby Day explains how to overcome
these and other common obstacles to publication.

She shows how to identify a suitable journal and how to plan, prepare and compile
a paper or article that will satisfy its requirements. She pays particular attention
to the creative aspects of the process. As an experienced journal editor Dr Day
is well placed to reveal the inside workings of the reviewing procedure – and
the more fully you understand this the greater the chance that what you submit
will finally be accepted.

For academic and research staff, in whatever discipline, a careful study
of Dr Day's book could be your first step on the road to publication.

GOWER

Your Student Research Project

Martin Luck

Now that you are approaching the final stages of your degree, have you ever wondered how you're going to cope with writing your dissertation? Apart from the practicalities of suddenly having to think and work in a completely different, and more in-depth, way than ever before, how are you going to fit it in with the rest of your work and also have a social life? *Your Student Research Project* will show you how.

This book gives you practical advice on how to cope with your project and make a success of your studies. It:

- is written in clear, accessible language
- provides a clear outline of practical guidance on how to run your project, from thinking about what topic to cover to the most effective way of presenting it
- explains how to work with your supervisor and the other important people around you
- shows you how to squeeze the maximum value from the effort you put in
- enables you to recognize how you have changed in the process
- encourages you to exploit the skills and experiences you have gained in the world beyond your degree.

It takes a different approach to other books on research methods because it considers the project as only one part of your existence. It concentrates on advice, ideas and examples while still giving thought to how you will manage your work within a crowded and exciting life. Above all, *Your Student Research Project* helps you to keep track of where you are heading and to make the right preparations for the future.

GOWER